What the critics say about

THE BEST OF THE BRITISH VIRGIN ISLANDS

"If you want to see the <u>real</u> British Virgin Islands, this book is for you...offers a near-guarantee of a great trip."
—*Independent Publisher*

"The Best of the British Virgin Islands is essential to getting the most out of any trip to the British Virgin Islands."
—*Midwest Book Review*

"The authors share intimate knowledge of hotels, inns, bars, restaurants, shops and attractions."
—*Virgin Islands Weekly Journal*

"Unquestionably the best guidebook ever written on the British Virgin Islands."
—*Peter Island Morning Sun*

"Insider tips and travel secrets."
—*Islands Magazine*

THE BEST OF THE BRITISH VIRGIN ISLANDS

Fourth Edition

PAMELA ACHESON
RICHARD B. MYERS

TWO THOUSAND THREE ASSOCIATES
TTTA

Published by
TWO THOUSAND THREE ASSOCIATES
4180 Saxon Drive, New Smyrna Beach, Florida 32169
Phone: 386.423.7523

Printed in the United States of America

Library of Congress Cataloging-in-Publication Data

Acheson, Pamela.
    The best of the British Virgin Islands / Pamela Acheson,
    Richard B. Myers . — 4th
    ed.
      p.   cm.
    ISBN 13: 9781892285119
    1. British Virgin Islands—Guidebooks.   I. Title
    F2129.A63   1997
    917.297'2504--dc21   97-44960
                                CIP

Photo Credits
Front Cover: Pamela Acheson. Leverick Bay, Virgin Gorda
Back Cover: Pamela Acheson. White Bay, Jost Van Dyke

ISBN-13 9781892285119
ISBN-10 1892285118

10 9 8 7 6 5 4

For Auntie Bea

TABLE OF CONTENTS

"Silver bird fly me away
to where the winter's warm
and the sea breezes
blow through the night"

—from Island Blues
by Quito Rymer

"I never met a place
like this in my life."

—Author Hugh Benjamin,
upon his arrival to the BVI

MAPS

The maps in this book are simply meant to be "locator maps" and are provided to show the general location of landmarks, restaurants, hotels, etc. When you arrive in the BVI, you will find excellent, extremely detailed large fold-out maps of the islands that are free and are available at car rental agencies, your hotel, tourist board offices, and elsewhere. If you want detailed maps before your trip, log on to www.caribbean-on-line.com.

ACKNOWLEDGMENTS

Special thanks to Jon Corhern at Imagecraft Designs.

DISCLAIMER

The authors have made every effort to ensure accuracy in this book. Neither the authors nor the publisher is responsible for anyone's traveling or vacation experiences.

INTRODUCTION

The Best of the British Virgin Islands, Fourth Edition, is a labor of love. We have been traveling to the Virgin Islands for over 30 years and have been residents of the British Virgin Islands on and off for almost 20 years.

We have had the pleasure of watching many repeat visitors fall in love with the BVI just the way we did. We wrote this book to try to help every visitor—even the first-time visitor—enjoy the very best these wonderful islands have to offer.

You'll notice some special features in the book called "Things people usually wish they had known sooner." Well, in a way, that is what this whole book is all about. We hope our years of island experiences not only offer the very best of the BVI to the reader, but also help everyone avoid the possible pitfalls and problems of traveling to an unfamiliar place.

The book is arranged alphabetically by island, and covers every topic, from places to stay to restaurants and snorkel trips. We hope it helps you make educated decisions on everything from where to go, what to do, and how to have the most fun—for you. An appendix in the back of the book provides ferry schedules and other practical information.

The British Virgin Islands are special. We hope when you visit you leave your footprints on dozens of deserted beaches and bring home many special memories.

Enjoy them and have fun!

— P.A. and R.B.M.

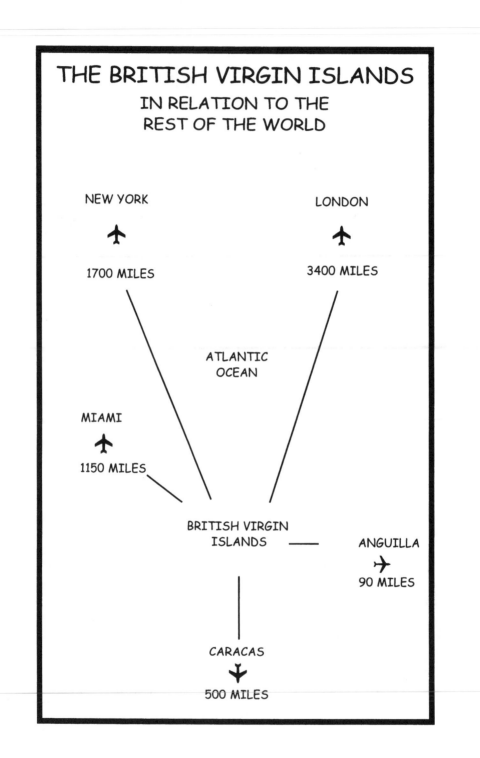

1. THE BRITISH VIRGIN ISLANDS

What are they?
They are a stunningly beautiful collection of 50 or so islands, islets, and cays that, with the exception of Anegada, are incredibly close together. Most are mountainous and steep-sided, some are rocky, and many are fringed with white-sand, crescent-shaped beaches. Except for the coral atoll of Anegada, all are volcanic in origin.

Where are they?
In the Caribbean, about 1700 miles southeast of New York City and 1150 miles southeast of Miami. They are 60 miles east of Puerto Rico and about 90 miles slightly northwest of Anguilla. Sombrero, an uninhabited island, sits halfway between the BVI and Anguilla.

Where are the BVI in relation to the USVI?
Right next to each other! The BVI and the USVI share the same archipelago, or group of islands: the USVI have the western half and the BVI the eastern half, with some overlapping in the middle. Some shorelines of the USVI and BVI lie less than half a mile apart.

How are the BVI different from the USVI?
Despite the close shorelines, stepping into the BVI from the USVI is like traveling to a faraway country. The atmosphere is completely different. The USVI population is almost 110,000 and two million tourists head there annually. There are stoplights and traffic jams. Only about 23,000 people live in all of the BVI. It's an entire country where almost everyone knows everyone else. Resorts are small and there aren't many (there are fewer hotel rooms in the BVI than in the Grand Hyatt Hotel in Manhattan). There is little nightlife. Although the cuisine is delicious, there are only a handful of sophisticated restaurants. The British Virgin Islands are quiet and remote and the U.S. and the USVI seem a million miles away.

What can you do in the BVI?

Walk deserted, dazzling, white-sand beaches. Drive to spectacular mountaintop vistas. Swim, snorkel, and dive in astonishingly clear, calm water. Horseback ride. Hike in the mountains. Sail in exceptionally protected waters. Go deep-sea fishing. Windsurf (locals travel island to island this way!). Or learn to do any of these things. You can also relax, or read, or rest. Or just sit very still and look around you and drink in the view and the soft island breezes. The BVI offer peace, quiet, and a slower pace. The BVI people are warm and friendly. These are the islands to come to for uninhabited beaches. Deserted snorkeling places. Bays where no one else is anchored. This is a place you can take in at your own speed, without crowds of other people blocking your view.

What's special about the BVI?

Everything! One of the BVI's greatest assets is its truly spectacular scenery, above the water and below. There are breathtaking mountaintop panoramas, stunning sunrises and sunsets, beaches that will steal your heart, water in countless unreproducible shades of blue. Below the water line is another magnificent world with great wrecks to dive around and scuba and snorkel areas so full of gaudily decorated fish that it will make you laugh.

Do the islands in the BVI differ from one another?

Absolutely! Despite the fact that the British Virgin Islands are lumped together as the "BVI," each island is actually very different, with its own unique character. When you've seen one, you definitely have not seen them all.

How easy is it to visit several British Virgin Islands?

The BVI is the only place in the entire Caribbean where so many islands are so close together. Many are only three or four miles from each other. Since it's all one country, it's incredibly easy to travel from island to island. Once you've cleared customs into the BVI, you are free to hop from one island to another, without paying departure and arrival taxes, going through customs, or lugging suitcases around. To get from island to island, you can go on a day sail, rent your own little motor boat, or take a public ferry.

2. EACH ISLAND IN A NUTSHELL

All of the British Virgin Islands are hilly and close together except very flat and far-flung Anegada. All are wonderful but each one is unbelievably different from all the others. Each one has a special character all its own.

Anegada is an eleven-mile-long, flat coral atoll surrounded by reefs. It's the northernmost of the BVI and lies barely above sea level about 15 miles north of Virgin Gorda. Only 211 people live on the island. There are very few places to stay and only a handful of extremely simple restaurants but there are miles of deserted beaches, great bonefishing and deep-sea fishing, and some of the best snorkeling in the world.

Beef Island is just 600 feet off Tortola's East End and a short bridge connects the two islands. Beef Island is where the Tortola airport is actually located (which always confuses first-time visitors — "Why am I flying to Beef Island?") and it's also where the ferries leave for Pusser's Marina Cay or Virgin Gorda's North Sound. Beef Island has a nice beach, a windsurfing school, some little shops, some eateries, a number of villas for rent, and a lovely little villa complex.

Cooper Island is five miles south of Tortola. It's a small island favored by the charter yacht crowd because of the large number of available moorings, the calm anchorage, and the popular open-air restaurant. The island also has several inhabitants, some rental villas, and a simple but charming 12-room inn.

Ginger Island is uninhabited and six miles southeast of Tortola.

Great Camanoe Island is just north of Beef Island and has a small number of residents.

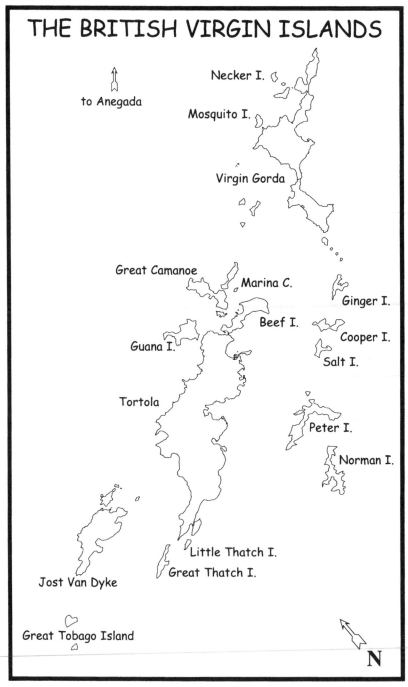

THE BRITISH VIRGIN ISLANDS

to Anegada

Necker I.

Mosquito I.

Virgin Gorda

Great Camanoe

Marina C.

Ginger I.

Beef I.

Cooper I.

Guana I.

Salt I.

Tortola

Peter I.

Norman I.

Little Thatch I.

Great Thatch I.

Jost Van Dyke

Great Tobago Island

N

Guana Island is a large and very hilly private island just north of Tortola's East End. The entire island is a remarkable nature preserve and also the setting for a small resort.

Jost Van Dyke is a hilly four-mile-long island five miles northwest of Tortola with 182 inhabitants and beachfront restaurants and bars. Two excellent anchoring harbors (three in the summer when White Bay swells lessen) and Foxy's famous Tamarind Bar make the island a "must stop" for just about everyone visiting the BVI. There are a few places to stay overnight and this island also makes a really great day trip from Tortola.

Little Thatch is a small, hilly island, and privately owned. There is one cottage for rent.

Marina Cay is an islet just north of Beef Island and is home to tiny Pusser's Marina Cay Resort, Pusser's Marina Cay Restaurant, and Pusser's Company Store, plus 35 moorings just offshore.

Mosquito Island is a half-mile-square island that is privately owned and borders North Sound just north of Virgin Gorda. The island has several lovely beaches and is very hilly.

Necker Island is a luxurious private retreat a mile and a half north of Virgin Gorda.

Norman Island is five miles south of Tortola and is uninhabited (except for several herds of goats). It's a favorite anchoring spot and features two restaurants, one on the beach and one floating offshore. Some of the BVI's best snorkeling is just off this island.

Peter Island is a four-and-a-half-mile-long, private island five miles south of Tortola with a 52-room resort nestled against its north shore. Ferry service is available from just outside Road Town for those wishing to use the beaches or dine there.

Saba Rock is a spit of an islet just 200 yards offshore of Virgin Gorda in North Sound. This tiny bit of land sports an eight-room resort, a popular restaurant, a large gift shop, and a number of moorings.

Salt Island is four miles south of Tortola and uninhabited. Its salt ponds were once the BVI's source of salt. Older residents remember boating here to pick up the family's salt supply, necessary for preserving food.

Scrub Island is a bit east of Great Camanoe and has just a few residents and a small restaurant. A resort is in the works.

Tortola, which is geographically in the center of the BVI, is also the largest, the hilliest, and by far the most populated island, with around 19,000 people. Although quiet by U.S. standards, this is the busiest island in the BVI and has the BVI's only real town, Road Town. Stores, bars, restaurants, and pubs are mixed in with government offices in Road Town and it can be busy here. Most places to stay are on the western end of Tortola, especially along the western north shore beaches. There are beautiful beaches along the entire north shore and miles of roads that are astonishingly steep in places and show off awesome views.

Virgin Gorda lies about eight miles east of Tortola, is physically a third smaller, and has a population of only 3,174. The island has one big mountain in the middle that separates two long and slender ends. Although one road crosses over the mountain, the two ends are really two separate destinations, each with its own small number of resorts, shops, and restaurants as well as beautiful beaches. Virgin Gorda's southern section descends into a flat and fairly arid tip with giant boulders scattered about. This is the location of the famous Baths. The northern end of Virgin Gorda, along with the shores of several smaller islands, almost completely encircles calm North Sound, creating an exceptionally protected body of water that is excellent for water sports. Four resorts, three right on Virgin Gorda and one on an islet, and all but one accessible only by boat, are scattered around the hilly North Sound shores.

George Dog, Fallen Jerusalem, and Round Rock are the delightful names of some of the BVI's uninhabited islands. Many have stunning beaches and snorkeling spots which you can reach easily by renting a powerboat or joining a group trip. Keep an eye out for the descriptive names of points and bays, such as the "Inaccessibles" on Mosquito Island or "Cow Wreck Beach" on Anegada.

16

3. ANEGADA

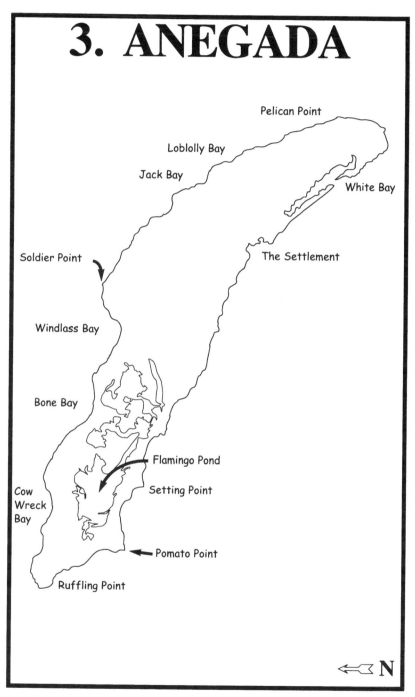

Pelican Point

Loblolly Bay

Jack Bay

White Bay

Soldier Point

The Settlement

Windlass Bay

Bone Bay

Flamingo Pond

Cow
Wreck
Bay

Setting Point

Pomato Point

Ruffling Point

N

ANEGADA

Anegada is a flat coral atoll 16 miles north of Virgin Gorda which is almost entirely surrounded by treacherous reefs. Snorkelers and divers love Anegada but it definitely can be a sailor's nightmare. There are well over 300 wrecks just offshore. In fact, although the channels are better marked than they used to be, charter companies don't allow their boats to be taken to Anegada without a captain. The approach to the anchorages takes a great deal of skill and local knowledge.

Only about 211 people live on Anegada and there are just a few places to stay, including a little hotel, a guest house, and a villa or two. There are a small number of very simple restaurants, and 26 miles of stunning white-sand beach. The island itself is plain and pleasant, but the underwater scenery is spectacular. Exquisite coral formations shimmering with colorful fish begin just inches from shore. You can snorkel here in very calm, clear water and you can swim to one coral grouping after another, for hours and hours. Anegada is also a place to come for excellent deep-sea fishing and superb bonefishing.

Staying on Anegada is a remarkably relaxing experience. There is "nothing" to do here. Take a picnic to a deserted area of beach or have lunch at a little beach restaurant. Spend the day snorkeling, or kayaking, or perhaps snoozing with a book in your lap. See if you can spot the elusive Anegada rock iguana. Or look for pink flamingos in the salt ponds (there are over 50 of these marvelous birds now living on Anegada). In the evening catch a stunning sunset and then dine on delicious local lobster. At night, spend hours looking up at the canopy of glittering stars.

If for some reason you develop island fever, you can always take a day trip over to Tortola.

GETTING TO ANEGADA

There are no scheduled flights to Anegada but **Caribbean Wings** *(284.495.6000)* or **Air Sunshine** *(284.495.8900)* can fly you there from Beef Island/Tortola on your schedule. **Smith's Ferry** *(284.494.4454, 284.494.2355)* runs ferries between Anegada and Road Town on Tortola and The Valley on Virgin Gorda *(see ferry schedules page 138).*

AIR AND BOAT TRIPS TO ANEGADA FOR THE DAY

Anegada is also a wonderful destination for a day trip. **Fly BVI** *(284.495.1747)* offers a package trip for $145 per person, minimum of four, that includes a tour of the island and lunch at the Big Bamboo. For boat trips to Anegada see Boat Trips from Tortola *(page 73)*, Boat Trips from Virgin Gorda *(pages 111 and 124)*, or call **Speedy's** *(284.495.5240)*.

GETTING AROUND

Tony's Taxi *(284.495.8027)* will take you on a tour around the island or drop you at a beach. **ABC Car Rentals** *(284.495.9466)* rents jeeps for about $65 a day or about $360 a week, plus fuel.

RESTAURANTS

Anegada Reef Hotel Restaurant *(284.495.8002)*, at Setting Point, cooks up outstanding grilled lobster, chicken, ribs, steak, and fish dinners which are served by candlelight. Drop by at lunch for a great lobster salad or a burger or a sandwich. *BLD $$*

Big Bamboo *(284.495.2019)* is right on beautiful Loblolly Bay beach near Jack Bay Point. It's the place to come for a sweet Anegada lobster, Jamaican jerk chicken, and local conch or grilled snapper. *L (D on request) $$*

Cow Wreck Beach Bar and Grill *(284.495.9461)*, beachfront at Lower Cow Wreck Beach, serves lobster salad sandwiches, conch fritters, and burgers at lunch and fish, ribs, and lobster at dinner. *LD $$*

Flash of Beauty *(284.495.8014)* is a simple beach bar at Loblolly Bay East serving fresh Anegada lobster, grilled fish, and sandwiches. *LD $$*

Neptune's Treasure *(284.495.9439)*, near Setting Point, features dinners of local lobster, swordfish, tuna, and conch at this simple, indoor spot. At lunch, dine on burgers or sandwiches, or anything from the dinner menu. *BLD $$*

Lobster Trap *(284.495.9466)*, right at Pomato Point, offers al fresco dining on a covered terrace. Dine on ribs, chicken, fish, conch, or local lobster. *LD $$*

> *For many people, Lowell Wheatley and Anegada*
> *were one and the same.*
> *His death brings a lingering sadness to all who knew him.*
> *His memory brings a lingering smile.*

SHOPPING
Anegada Reef Hotel Boutique *(284.495.8002)* showcases stylish resortwear, local spices and relishes, island prints, original soaps, and excellent gift items.

Pat's Pottery and Art *(284.495.8031)* features mugs, plates and platters, pitchers, and bowls, all whimsically hand-painted in pastel colors.

Purple Turtle *(no phone)* is the place for T-shirts, gifts, and Internet access.

BONEFISHING, FLY-FISHING, AND DEEP-SEA FISHING
Cast from the beach or get a kayak for tarpon, snook, and jacks. Or take a day trip with a local guide and reel in a gamefish. **Anegada Reef Hotel** *(284.495.8002)* offers bonefishing trips. A half-day is $275.

WHERE TO STAY
Anegada Reef Hotel is the island's only hotel and it is very informal and delightfully laid back. If the bartender is not around, you make a drink and write down what you had. Meal hours, special trips, and messages are casually scribbled on a blackboard daily. Rooms are on the spare side, but comfortable. The hotel is on a strand of sand on the south side of the island, but snorkelers and beach lovers will want to spend their days on the deserted and gorgeous beach that runs for miles along the island's spectacular north shore. If you prefer to rent your own house, **Setting Point Villa** is an air-conditioned, four-bedroom, three-bath villa on two acres a short stroll down the beach from the hotel.
20 rooms. Rates for two people, including meals: $250-$275 a night plus 15% service charge and 7% government tax ($215-$250 off-season). Villa $500 ($400). Tel: 284.495.8002. Fax: 284.495.9362. www.anegadareef.com

Lavenda Breeze is Anegada's only other real villa. It sits all by itself on the north coast of Anegada, on beautiful Loblolly Bay. The beach plus swimming and snorkeling are right out your door. There are three bedrooms, a fully equipped kitchen, a comfortable deck that wraps completely around the house, satellite TV, and a VCR. Full provisioning can be arranged.
Weekly rates: $2,975 plus 7% government tax. Tel: 888.868.0199. Fax: 407.268.9869. www.lavendabreeze.com

Neptune's Treasure, on the south side of the island between Pomato Point and Setting Point, has simple air-conditioned rooms, each with a private bath on a narrow strip of beach.
9 rooms. Rates: $105 a night plus 10% for maid service (on request) plus 7% government tax for two people ($95 off-season). Tel: 284.495.9439. Fax: 284.495.8060. www.neptunestreasure.com

SNORKELING HINTS

❑ When you are snorkeling, never ever touch anything. Sea urchins (those round, black things with thin, black spikes sticking up) and certain corals can sting badly.

❑ Also, never ever stand on anything but sand. Coral reefs are exceptionally fragile and grow incredibly slowly. What you destroy with a single crunch of your flipper will take years to replace.

❑ To really see what is going on around a reef, try to hover and stare at one particular section. At first you may notice just a few things. But keep looking. The longer you look at one spot, the more activity you'll see.

❑ If your mask keeps fogging up, rinse it in the sea water, spit onto the inside, rub the spit all around the glass, rinse the mask briefly, and put it back on. Or buy a defogger (but the spit works equally well and you are less likely to run out).

❑ If you forgot your prescription mask (or didn't even know you could get one), you can buy them in the BVI at almost any dive shop.

SNORKELING IN THE BVI

The waters around the BVI look incredibly peaceful. But stick your head below the surface and you'll see that there's an amazing amount of stuff going on down there.

Even if you don't really like to swim, consider snorkeling in the BVI at least once. The water is astonishingly clear, there are great shipwrecks to explore, and the millions of brightly colored fish are amazing to see.

Trying to point out the best snorkeling places in the BVI would be sort of like trying to list good French restaurants in Paris. The waters around the British Virgin Islands are teeming with fish—everywhere, right up to the very shoreline.

In fact, if you stand anywhere along the water's edge and drop in broken-up bits of stale rolls, it will only be a minute or two before fish will show up to eat. Sometimes the fish will nibble right out of your hand!

How to Snorkel

Snorkeling is something even the most timid soul can try. You can just wade in from the beach with a snorkel and mask and stick your head underwater. Most beaches have excellent snorkeling areas at one or both ends, or wherever a reef has grown. You can also go on organized snorkeling trips all over the BVI.

The truly decadent snorkelers simply lie down on one of those brightly colored yellow floats and stick their head over the edge!

Snorkeling over Sand

You can snorkel almost anywhere, and beginners are sometimes most comfortable just wading into calm water from the beach and snorkeling over the sand. You'll get to see some fish and you can look for rays, which are the color of the sand and almost impossible to see unless they decide to move. You can also look for turtles and sand dollars.

Snorkeling over Reefs

The most colorful sea creatures cluster around reefs. It's here that you will see fish, some much smaller than an inch, in all manner of gaudy costumes: bold white and orange stripes, bright purple speckled with silver stars, iridescent stripes of blue and chartreuse. But it's not just the reef fish that are colorful. So is the reef. Watch for the many types of coral. Look for sponges and sea anemones and starfish. And look around you in the water. A great sight to catch is a family of baby squid, each less than half an inch in length, hanging still in a perfect row.

Great Reefs and Great Snorkeling Trips

You can find colorful reefs just offshore of virtually every BVI beach. Or you can take a boat trip to a great snorkeling spot (see pages 73, 111, and 124).

VISITING THE USVI FOR A DAY

The USVI and the BVI are right next to each other and yet so very different. It can be fun to head to St. John or St. Thomas for the day. Don't forget your passport!

ST. JOHN

The shoreline of St. John is just a few miles south of Tortola's West End. It's a pleasant 40-minute boat ride and you get a chance to explore a completely different island. St. John is mostly a national park. You can hike trails that lead to beautiful beaches and to petroglyphs, wander around the tiny town of Cruz Bay, and browse through little Mongoose Junction, one of the prettiest shopping complexes in the Caribbean. Ferries leave West End, Tortola, at 9:15 am and you can come back as late as 5 pm on Friday, 4:30 pm on Sunday, or 3:30 pm the other days. The round-trip fare is $35. Call Inter-Island Boat Services *(284.495.4166)*.

ST. THOMAS

St. Thomas is only four miles west of the West End of Tortola and you can take a ferry to downtown Charlotte Amalie where there are many shops and restaurants. On Tortola, ferries leave from Road Town and West End. Fares are $45 round-trip from either place. Call Fast Ferry *(284.494.2323)*, Smith's Ferry *(284.495.4495)* or Native Son *(284.495.4617)* for schedules. The boat ride takes about 45 minutes from West End to downtown St. Thomas. Speedy's *(284.495.5240)* also makes the run between The Valley in Virgin Gorda and downtown St. Thomas but it's an hour and a half each way. On Saturdays you can leave at 8:30 am and catch the 3:30 pm ferry back.

4. COOPER

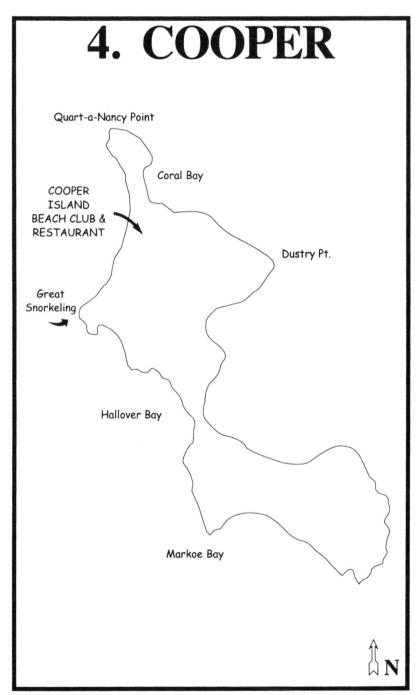

Quart-a-Nancy Point

Coral Bay

COOPER
ISLAND
BEACH CLUB &
RESTAURANT

Dustry Pt.

Great
Snorkeling

Hallover Bay

Markoe Bay

N

COOPER

Cooper Island is a small but hilly island that has long been popular with the charter boat crowd. There's a little beach and some outstanding snorkeling. There's also a casual restaurant, a nice little barefoot bar, a boutique, a dive shop, some rental houses (www.cooperisland.com), and a little informal resort. And that's it! There are no roads or cars on this island and only about six people live here.

The Cooper Island Beach Club is a great getaway. Even though it's isolated, every night you can meet a new group of people at the bar who have anchored for the night. It's kind of fun to be a "local" and watch people come and go. If you want to visit Tortola for the day, hop on the ferry Monday, Wednesday, and Friday (see schedule page 138). Each week on season there is a scheduled trip to Virgin Gorda. If you want to come here just for the day, rent a boat or take a boat trip (see pages 73, 111, 124).

Cooper Island Restaurant *(VHF Channel 16)* has been here for years. It's an informal open-air place which looks out over the bay. For lunch you can get hamburgers, conch fritters, soup and salad, a grilled vegetable sandwich, and superb ratatouille (luckily, the ratatouille is also offered as an appetizer for dinner). Evening specialties include barbecued chicken breast, conch creole, grilled mahi mahi, and penne pasta with chicken or shrimp. The bar is truly barefoot, and it's open all day. *LD (continental breakfast for hotel guests) $$*

The **Cooper Island Beach Club** is a very compact but surprisingly private place that is ultra-casual, quite relaxing, and slightly like camping. Six duplex West Indian-style yellow cottages are hidden among the palm trees just 50 feet from a little beach. All units are on the second floor (the first floor is storage and cistern) and views look out through tropical foliage. Units are small and modestly furnished, but appealing. All have little kitchens with gas stoves, outdoor showers, ceiling fans (no air-conditioning), tape decks, and balconies. Water is from rain stored in the cistern (use it sparingly). There is no electricity plant on the island, and lights, ceiling fans, and tape deck are powered by a 12-volt DC set-up in each room (a 110-volt outlet can be used to power up batteries in the evening when the generator is on). Shorts, T-shirts, and bathing suit are all you'll need. Bring groceries from Road Town or request provisioning. Manager Curt Berkley is always around and extremely helpful.
12 rooms. Rates: $195 plus 17% tax and service per night for two people ($135 spring, fall; $105 summer). Res: 800.542.4624. Tel: 413.863.3162. Local Tel: 284.495.9084. Fax: 413.863.3662. www.cooper-island.com

HELPFUL HINTS

❑On the BVI, as on many islands, people exchange greetings and inquire about each other's health before getting down to business. This is true whether they run into a friend, stop for gas, go to the grocery store, visit the bank, or order food at a restaurant. It's considered very rude to skip this conversational step. So start with a "Hello, how are you doing today?" and have a little introductory conversation. (Actually you'll find this "politeness" is much appreciated stateside also.)

❑In these islands, when you didn't hear what someone said, the polite way to ask for a repeat is to say "Say again?" or "Please repeat" rather than "What?"

❑It may puzzle you that sometimes you can't always understand the British Virgin Islanders even though they are speaking English. This is not just because of the West Indian accent. It is also because the idioms are different. In the States, you "go for a swim," didn't "hear" something, "turn" a latch, "put" it down, say "Yes." Islanders "take a sea bath," didn't "catch" something, "swing" a latch, "rest" it, and say "It would seem so." A list of all the idiomatic differences would fill a book.

❑Most islanders are actually going out of their way to talk "your language" when they talk to you. They are speaking extra slowly and avoiding the local phrases that seem to most confuse visitors. (Try listening to a group of islanders chatting among themselves and you'll see how much faster and more idiomatically they talk.) Also, the accent varies from Jost to Tortola to Virgin Gorda.

THINGS PEOPLE USUALLY WISH THEY HAD KNOWN SOONER

❑**Bugs.** Keep a little container of bug repellent (like a Cutter stick) with you at all times. This is actually a good idea if you are traveling anywhere in the Caribbean. It's not that any place is always buggy, it just can be buggy practically anywhere when there is absolutely no breeze.

❑**Itchy bug bites.** If you get bitten and have nothing to stop the itch, remember that a dab of straight gin or vodka usually works (you're supposed to apply it directly to the bite, but some people swear it works just as well if you drink it instead).

❑**Soap but no water.** When you are in a washroom in the BVI (or, in fact, almost anywhere in the Caribbean), check that water will actually come out of the faucet before you put that liquid soap on your hands. It's tough to get it off if there's no water around. (It can be handy to carry antibacterial handwash with you.)

❑**Missing meals.** If you are flying from the States to the BVI via Puerto Rico, you will discover that connections can make it impossible to eat for many hours so tuck some food and a bottle of water (if it's allowed) in your carryon.

❑**Holidays.** On major public holidays *(see Appendix)*, almost everything in the BVI closes up.

❑**ATMs.** Most BVI banks have them but they rarely work, so don't count on getting cash this way.

5. GUANA

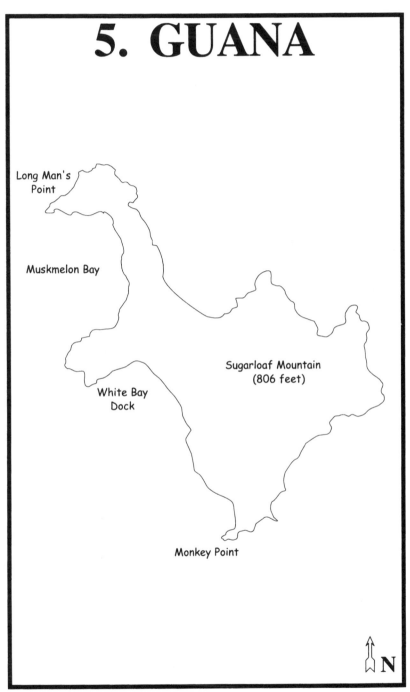

Long Man's
Point

Muskmelon Bay

White Bay
Dock

Sugarloaf Mountain
(806 feet)

Monkey Point

N

GUANA

Guana, at 850 acres, is the seventh largest British Virgin Island. It is extremely hilly and very private and home to the Guana Island resort. All of the island is a nature preserve and wildlife and bird sanctuary and there are rare roseate flamingos, masked boobys, and frigate birds, and many kinds of herons. At least 50 species of birds are regularly found there. Scientists from several academic institutions are engaged in ongoing studies of Guana Island's flora and fauna.

Peaceful paths meander through lush tropical greenery and brilliant flowering bushes and trees. There are seven usually empty beaches and lots of hiking trails (some quite strenuous) that go all over the island. Staying here is a one-of-a-kind experience. It is simple, civilized, and can be very relaxing. The island is truly private. The dining room and other facilities are not open to outside guests and there are no day-trippers on the island (except sometimes at the beaches—all beaches in the BVI are public).

The **Guana Island** resort is perched on the top of one of Guana Island's hills and there are astonishingly beautiful panoramic views in every direction. Appealing rooms, most in cottages with handsome stone walls and beamed ceilings, are simply decorated but comfortable. Many have separate sitting areas and all have porches or balconies and private entrances. None have phones, but all are wi-fi. Breakfast, lunch, and dinner are served on stone terraces and guests often sit together. The drawing room is a gathering place for before-dinner cocktails. Dinner is a casually elegant affair and guests generally dine together at several large tables and join in the evening conversation.

There are seven beautiful and usually deserted beaches, a little honor beach bar, good snorkeling areas, tennis courts, and various water activities and therapeutic massage (in your room or on the beach) are available. Hiking trails lead to beaches and secluded vistas. You can spend days hiking and swimming or reclined on the beach or your private terrace absorbed in a book or just taking in the views. This can be a remarkably relaxing place.

15 units. Rates (all meals, house wines with lunch and dinner, and use of all equipment): $895-$1,095 for two people ($650-$775 off-season). North Beach Cottage $1,500 ($1,200 off-season) plus 17% tax and service. Closed Sept., Oct. Res: 800.544.8262. Tel: 914.967.6050. Local tel: 284.494.2354. Fax: 914.967.8048. Web: www.guana.com

SO, DID YOU KNOW THAT. . .?

❑ If you pushed all the British Virgin Islands together into one land mass, it would cover only 59 square miles. That's about the same size as Nantucket Island. Or one-twentieth the size of Rhode Island, the smallest state in the union.

❑ William Thornton, who designed the U.S. Capitol building, was born in the BVI in 1759 on the island of Jost Van Dyke.

❑ Only about 23,000 people live in the BVI. Seven times this number of people live in Stamford, Connecticut. And twice this many people live in Beverly Hills, California. If everybody in the BVI (the whole entire country) took a seat in the new Yankee stadium, well . . . the stadium would still be more than half empty!

❑ Latitudinally, the BVI are located roughly halfway between the equator and New York City.

❑ It's only about 10 degrees warmer in the summer than in the winter in the BVI. Winter temperatures average about 75 degrees, summer about 85 degrees.

❑ If you headed directly east from the BVI, you would eventually be in the Sahara Desert. As a matter of fact, in the BVI in the summer the air is sometimes hazy because it is full of Sahara dust, fine particles of sand that have been blown by the trade winds all the way from Africa. You can actually feel a fine layer of grittiness on the surface of things.

❑ The wind in the BVI generally blows in the opposite direction from the winds that sweep across the United States and Europe. On these continents, the wind and the weather generally come from the west. In the BVI, the wind and the weather generally come out of the east.

❑ The BVI really does have seasons. Although it rarely ever rains for long, in the winter there are more frequent two-minute cloudbursts (which keep the hills emerald green), the humidity is low, and there are very steady trade winds. Summer is frequently dry (the hills can turn brown), more humid, and less windy. It can also be hazy when a tropical wave is passing through.

❑ The Christmas winds, which usually start (you guessed it) just around Christmas, are strong and sometimes stay at 30 to 40 knots for several days, or even several weeks.

❑ The flat road on Tortola that runs between Road Town and West End wasn't built until 1966 when they reclaimed that flat land from the sea. As recently as 1965 it was an all-day trip by donkey from that end of the island to town! You'll still catch sight of old-timers traveling the old-fashioned way!

6. JOST VAN DYKE

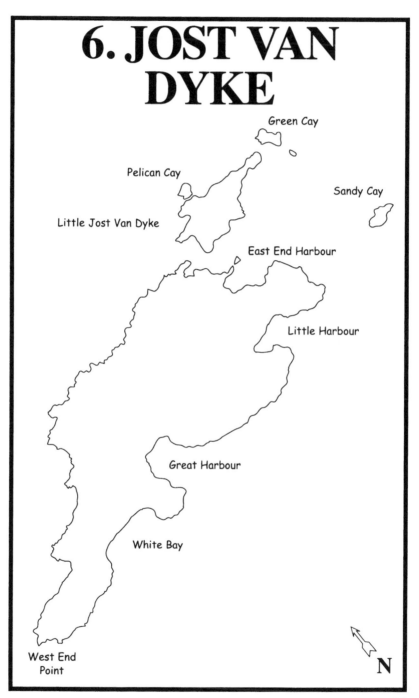

Green Cay

Pelican Cay

Sandy Cay

Little Jost Van Dyke

East End Harbour

Little Harbour

Great Harbour

White Bay

West End
Point

N

JOST VAN DYKE
IN A NUTSHELL

Jost Van Dyke is about five miles northwest of Tortola. It's four miles long, very hilly, and home to just 182 people. The island is known by yachters around the world for its gentle anchorages and for its delightful barefoot, beachfront bars, including the famous Foxy's, which is one of the most celebrated watering holes in the entire Caribbean.

Four tiny settlements are tucked along Jost's curvy southern and eastern shores: White Bay, Great Harbour, Little Harbour, and East End. A single road connects the settlements and then turns into a heart-stopping roller coaster as it loops up into the hills and over steep peaks.

There are only a few facilities for staying overnight (see pages 42-44). Most people either catch a ferry or rent a small powerboat and visit for the day or arrive on their own boat or on a charterboat and spend the night on water. Those that do stay on land have the opportunity to be incredibly laid-back and relaxed. There's virtually no contact with the outside world and no need to ever wear shoes, unless you decide to hike the road or the hills. If you get island fever, you can hop on a ferry and go to Tortola for the day.

WHAT YOU CAN DO ON JOST VAN DYKE

You can swim in calm waters, snorkel at secret spots, read, rest, bask in the sun, hike the hills, swim with dolphins and rays, go on spectacular diving trips, visit deserted beaches, snooze with no interruptions, gaze at glittering star-filled nighttime skies. Restaurants and bars are scattered along the water's edge and you can walk from one to another in a delightfully relaxed, "no shoes required" atmosphere.

GETTING TO JOST VAN DYKE FROM TORTOLA AND USVI

Ferries run between West End, Tortola and Great Harbour, Jost Van Dyke *(see schedule page 138)*. These ferries double as supply boats to Jost, so you may be sharing a seat with cases of soda and cartons and cartons of just about anything. Bear in mind that the boat may leave early or late, so get to the dock with time to spare. When someone begins to untie the lines, that means the boat is leaving, so hop aboard. Ferries also run from the USVI *(see schedule page 140)*.

EXPLORING JOST VAN DYKE

The only flat land on Jost Van Dyke is found along several curvy bays on the southern and eastern sides of the island and it is here that people settled, at Great Harbour, Little Harbour, White Bay, and East End Harbour. The island's single road forms a six-mile, curvy loop that runs up and down over seaside hills to connect the shoreline settlements and then heads up across the peaks of the uninhabited part of the island to show off stunning views. Driving this road is a delightful adventure.

Between the settlements, the road is mostly paved and, although quite steep in places, is easily driveable. However, the section of road that takes off into the mountains is very rough (it's sometimes crushed rock, sometimes dirt, and occasionally grass), breathtakingly steep, and contains some unforgettable hairpin turns. It also provides spectacular views of the shoreline below and of sea and nearby islands as it twists and turns across virgin hills, so be sure to bring a camera. This long section of the road is little traveled and it is rare to encounter another car or even to see another person.

If you prefer not to take the whole road, there is a shortcut up to it just to the west of Rudy's Suprette. When you get to the top, turn left for the short version, and right for the long. If you want to leave the driving to someone else, hire a taxi for a tour.

Steep hills separate the settlements and you will want to rent a jeep or hire a taxi or travel by water taxi. Hardy souls can walk from Great Harbour to White Bay. It takes a good 15 minutes just to get over the hill (a real killer in the afternoon sun) to the very eastern edge of White Bay beach. Then it's another 10 minutes along the sand and over some rocks to the beach bars at the western end of White Bay.

There are many great snorkeling spots on Jost Van Dyke, including the rocky areas of White Bay and the East End beaches. Or you can take a little boat to the north side of Little Jost Van Dyke for excellent snorkeling. You can also take a little boat to a number of deserted beaches on nearby cays. Don't miss the "bubbly hole" on East End. When the waves are up, it can be pretty explosive! Scuba diving, sport-fishing, eco-tours, hiking trips on deserted islands, and much more can be easily arranged.

Renting a jeep

You can rent a jeep from Sendrick Chinnery at **Paradise Jeep Rentals** *(284.495.9477 or 496.8326)* for about $50 a day.

Hiring a taxi

Bun *(284.499.8871)*, Claude *(284.443.4178)*, Greg *(284.499.5127)* and Abe *(284.496.8429)* drive taxis. Look for them by the Great Harbour Dock or near the Customs House or call (there's a pay phone near the Customs House). The fare from Great Harbour to White Bay or Little Harbour is about $5 per person.

Hiring a water taxi

Greg *(284.495.9401)* offers local water taxi service around Jost Van Dyke and also to other islands. **Dohm's Water Taxi** *(340.775.6501)* provides service between the USVI and the BVI on their stable, wave-piercing catamarans. The fare is $250 for up to five people (gratuity welcome) plus a $20 per person customs fee. They also offer transportation from one BVI to another.

Renting a dinghy or a boat or taking a boat trip

KC Boat Rentals *(284.496.8249, 284.495.9300)* has a 22' (220 hp) and a 28' (two 220 hp) Mako for charter. **BVI Eco-Tours** *(284.495.0271, 284.496.7603)* rents dinghies. Call **Captain Tony** *(284.495.0249)* for a trip to various islands on his 28' Sea Ray *Sundancer*.

Adventures for solo travelers, couples, and families

Snorkel rarely visited spots, hike deserted islands, swim with dolphins and sea turtles and rays, scuba virtually unexplored dive sites, experience open ocean blue water diving, learn to scuba, visit an amazing underwater room, bird watch, take a botanical walk, learn about the local flora and fauna on an eco-tour, and more. Just call **Jost Van Dyke Scuba** and **BVI Eco-Tours** *(284.495.0271, 284.496.7603)* to arrange the adventure of your dreams.

GREAT HARBOUR

Great Harbour, the most populated area of Jost Van Dyke, is a very small settlement, with casual bar-restaurants and shops scattered near the shore. The public dock, where the ferries tie up, is on the west side of the harbour and you can walk or taxi the short distance along the shore to "town." The water is good for swimming and snorkeling, but watch out for dinghies speeding about. By the way, when you are on the beach at Great Harbour looking out across the water, virtually all the distant hills you see are part of St. John (USVI).

GREAT HARBOUR SHOPPING

Christine's Bakery *(284.495.9281)* showcases delicious breads and rolls including coconut and banana bread, brownies, cakes, pies, and doughnuts—all freshly baked, plus her irresistible cinnamon and raisin sweet rolls.

Foxy's Boutique *(284.495.9275)* looks petite from the beach but inside you'll find one room keeps leading to another, and all are stocked with casual resortwear, colorful T-shirts, swimwear, shorts, CDs of island music (including Foxy's, naturally), books, postcards, sunscreen, batteries, a variety of unusual gift items, and a full line of Foxy's products, from playing cards to boxer shorts.

Ice House *(284.495.9263)*, which is at the end of the little road that goes past Christine's, is the place to go for ice—by the cube and by the block. Be sure to stop here for a bottle of Joyce Chinnery's outstanding mango chutney.

Jost Van Dyke Groceries *(284.495.0249)* is tucked in the back corner of a West Indian cottage, known as the "mini-mall." An ATM is here plus shelves jammed with everything from batteries to bottles of Chardonnay. An even bigger draw is Captain Tony and the sweet sound of his guitar.

Jost Van Dyke Ice Cream Parlor *(no phone)* offers ice cream in an assortment of flavors. It's at the front of the "mini-mall" across from Wendell's.

Nature's Basket *(284.495.3489)*, next to Christine's, features exquisite seasonal fruits grown up in the hills on Jost Van Dyke. Come here for deliciously sweet pineapples, papayas, mangoes, and bananas. You'll also find a small selection of vegetables, cheeses, eggs, canned goods, and sodas.

Rudy's Suprette *(284.495.9282)*, at the opposite end of the beach from Foxy's, carries canned goods, water, sodas, beer, and a variety of items which change depending on what the supply boat delivers. If you are looking for almost anything, there's a chance you'll find it here.

GREAT HARBOUR

Ice House
❑
❑Christine's Bakery
❑Nature's Basket
Rudy's   Customs
❑   Office
   Corsairs   ❑   JVD Ice Cream, JVD Groceries
    ❑   ❑
          Wendell's World❑   Foxy's❑
to Ferry Dock
                               Foxy's Dock

GREAT HARBOUR RESTAURANTS AND BARS

Ali Baba's *(284.495.9280)* offers burgers, conch fritters, and rotis plus an inviting bar. Don't miss the Monday night all-you-can-eat pig roast. *BLD $$*

Christine's Bakery *(284.495.9281)* is **the** place to come for breakfast. Sit on the terrace and dine on eggs and bacon, fresh fruit, freshly baked coconut bread, or Christine's exceptional cinnamon and raisin sweet rolls. *BLD $*

Corsairs *(284.495.9294)* decor is a mix of Caribbean and pirate paraphernalia. Crowds drop in for the chilled shots and specialty drinks (try the wicked Voodoo juice) and everyone stays for the food. At breakfast and lunch it's mostly Tex-Mex: breakfast burritos; seafood, chicken, and lobster quesadillas; chili with chips; plus burgers. At dinner, the menu turns Italian: pan-seared tuna with roasted eggplant, pasta primavera, seafood pomodoro, plus specials. *BLD $$*

Foxy's Tamarind Bar *(284.495.9258)* serves some of the very best food on the island and gallons and gallons of their irresistible painkiller punch, but the real draw here is Foxy himself, who is never without his guitar. He sings most afternoons and wanders in and out other times, happy to create impromptu, amusing ballads about his guests. Come here for a cold bottle of Foxy's own beer plus burgers and rotis for lunch, and grilled fish, steak, and lobster for dinner. Barbecues are Friday and Saturday evenings. Despite the immense popularity of this place, the atmosphere remains remarkably unhurried and pleasant, thanks to Foxy's wife, Tessa, and to the exceptionally professional staff. Check out the business cards stapled almost everywhere. Find anyone you know? *No food Sept. but bar is often open and you might find Foxy. LD $$*

Rudy's Mariner's Rendezvous *(284.495.9282)*, at the western end of the beach, has a popular bar and serves everything from burgers to lobster. *BLD $$*

Wendell's World *(284.495.9259)* is a casual spot for burgers, sandwiches, and fried chicken. *LD $$*

GREAT HARBOUR NIGHTLIFE

Corsairs *(284.495.9294)*. Local entertainers appear here some nights.

Foxy's Tamarind Bar *(284.495.9258)*. Foxy entertains many afternoons (except Sundays or if he's gone fishing). Live bands play Thursday, Friday, and Saturday nights (and Tuesday and Wednesday nights, on season). Some nights a DJ takes over. To find out what band is playing when you are visiting, pick up the current edition of the *Limin' Times* or go online to www.limin-times.com.

LITTLE HARBOUR

Little Harbour, a tiny settlement, is separated from Great Harbour by a large hill. It's a popular anchorage but there is virtually no beach. Several ultra-casual restaurants are right at the water's edge.

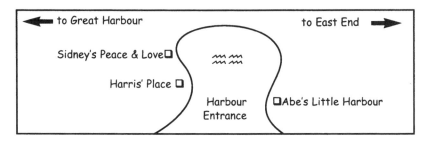

LITTLE HARBOUR SHOPPING

Abe's Little Harbour *(284.495.9329)* has a little grocery inside.

Sidney's Peace & Love *(284.495.9271)* has an outdoor boutique and sells cotton dresses, T-shirts, and more.

LITTLE HARBOUR RESTAURANTS AND BARS

Abe's Little Harbour *(284.495.9329)*, in a cottage on the eastern edge of the harbour, turns out delicious lobster, chicken, fish, conch, and spareribs for lunch and dinner and holds a pig roast Wednesday night on season. *BLD $$*

Harris' Place *(284.495.9302)*, painted pastel blue and purple, serves meals at picnic tables at the water's edge and cooks up full breakfasts plus hamburgers and sandwiches for lunch and West Indian-style fish and conch and lobster for dinner. There's a pig roast nightly in season. Call Cynthia to make a reservation for dinner. *BLD $$*

Sidney's Peace & Love *(284.495.9271)*, with an eclectic variety of tables spread across the dock out over the water and under a makeshift roof (which also serves as the display rack for numerous T-shirts) prepares breakfast daily and lobster, chicken, fish, and West Indian dishes for lunch and dinner. *BLD $$*

LITTLE HARBOUR NIGHTLIFE

Harris' Place *(284.495.9302)*. Ruben Chinnery plays his guitar and sings Monday nights.

Sidney's Peace & Love *(284.495.9271)*. Bands perform here on season.

WHITE BAY

White Bay has two long and lovely beaches, connected by a path that wends its way across an outcropping of rock. On the western beach is tiny Sandcastle Hotel, a handful of beach restaurants and bars, and a few beach boutiques. This is a popular day trip from St. Thomas in the USVI and this end of the beach can actually get extraordinarily crowded on weekend afternoons. East of the rock outcropping, just over the hill from Great Harbour, is Ivan's outstanding Stress-Free Bar, a little campground, and several villas.

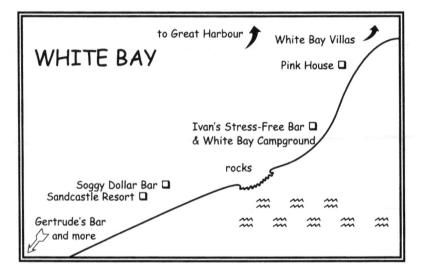

WHITE BAY SHOPPING

Ivan's Stress-Free Bar *(284.495.9358)* rents snorkel equipment and has a selection of used paperback books.

Sheniques Boutique *(no phone)*, on the beach west of Sandcastle, sells delightful island wear: colorful men's shirts, gauzy dresses, sarongs, T-shirts.

Sandcastle Resort Boutique *(284.495.9888)* features T-shirts, bathing suits, film, suntan lotion, and postcards.

Wendell's World Boutique *(no phone)* offers clothing, beachwear, and gifts.

White Bay Superette *(no phone)*, outlined in shells, carries numerous items: beer, chips, ice cream, suntan lotion, canned goods, cold sodas, and juices.

WHITE BAY RESTAURANTS, BARS, AND NIGHTLIFE

Gertrude's Beach Bar *(284.495.9104)* is a good choice for an icy cold beer or a frozen concoction, plus burgers for lunch and ribs or fish for dinner. *LD $$*

Ivan's Stress-Free Bar *(284.495.9358)* is tucked into the foliage along the eastern section of White Bay beach. There's a sandy veranda, a belly-up bar, and delightful decor: thousands of shells on the pastel-painted walls, ceiling, and entrance. Burgers, tuna melts, grilled cheese, and local beef or chicken pates are lunch fare. Every Thursday evening the locally famous guitarist Ruben entertains and Ivan throws a cookout barbecue (reservations by 4 pm essential!). Friday nights Elvis from Bequia entertains (and you can say you "saw Elvis on Jost Van Dyke"). Ivan's is the home of the International "All Stars Ever-Changing Band." Bring an instrument and join the festive jam session, which can occur almost any night. On some nights you can catch someone famous jamming away. It's a Kenny Chesney favorite. If no one shows up to jam, Ivan entertains solo. *L daily (D Thurs., reservations essential). $-$$*

Jewel's Shack *(no phone)* is a tiny place that specializes in burgers, hot dogs, and light snacks during the day. *L $*

One Love Beach Bar *(284.495.9829)* is decorated with a bevy of bouys and detritus washed up from the sea. It's at the east end of the beach and is a good stop for a tropical drink or an icy beer.

Sandcastle Restaurant's *(284.495.9888)* dinner is surprisingly and delightfully elegant, as tablecloths and candlelight magically transform what is known during the day as the Soggy Dollar Bar *(see below)*. The four-course menu changes nightly and includes a soup (such as butternut squash), a salad, and a tempting dessert plus a choice of three entrees, such as chicken cacciatore, grilled pork chop, or red snapper. Call after 10 am to find out the day's menu and, please, choose your entree before 4 pm. Dinner begins promptly at 7 pm. *Closed Mon. and Sept. Reservations essential by 4 pm. Prix fixe $35 plus 15%.*

Soggy Dollar Bar *(284.495.9888)* claims to be the originator of that smooth rum concoction known as the painkiller (check out the letter on the wall). Dine at lunch in your bathing suit on a juicy hamburger, a great flying fish sandwich, or tasty conch fritters. Order lunch at the bar and carry it to a table, the beach, or even a hammock. Breakfast is served from 9:15 to 10 am. It's packed here on Sunday afternoons when Ruben Chinnery strums his guitar and sings his very own renditions of popular ballads and soft rock. *No breakfast Sept. BL $$*

41

JOST VAN DYKE LODGING

There are only a handful of places to stay overnight on Jost Van Dyke. A tiny resort, several cottages and houses, and a campground are on White Bay. On remote East End you'll find a small collection of houses.

Don't come here looking for luxury. Life on Jost Van Dyke is extremely simple: no traffic, virtually no television, phones that work haphazardly, electricity that comes and goes. For those who can bear to be "unplugged" it's an outstandingly relaxing experience. You'll need very few clothes—a bathing suit plus some T-shirts and shorts. There are almost no laundry facilities, most air-conditioning is of the natural kind, water comes mostly from cisterns and must be used sparingly, and although the island was recently electrified, power outages are common.

What you get instead of modern conveniences are a fabulously laid-back atmosphere, nights of extraordinarily brilliant stars, a chance to just sit and watch the scenery change as the sun catches a wave or a sudden cloudburst momentarily obscures a nearby island and creates a staggeringly beautiful rainbow. On Jost Van Dyke you get the chance to really pause.

However, on Jost you are not completely isolated. Great Harbour and Little Harbour are two of the most popular anchorages in the BVI and boaters come ashore to dine. White Bay is hugely popular with day-trippers from the USVI and, especially on season, White Bay bars and beaches can be startlingly frenetic in the afternoon.

If you want you can join in the fun, knowing that in a few hours you will once again be experiencing the simplicity and peace of living on a relatively large island with fewer than 200 other people. If you want to avoid the afternoon crowds you can visit the bubbly pool at East End, hike the road, or have a water taxi drop you off on the beach of a nearby uninhabited island, or even take a day trip to Tortola. If you really want complete isolation, your best bet is Sandy Ground Estates at East End.

Note: If you are staying on Jost and arriving directly from St. Thomas, USVI, you must clear customs at the Customs Office at Great Harbour. Rates provided here are on season (off-season rates in parentheses) and do not include 7% hotel tax or 10% service charge.

SANDCASTLE HOTEL
Slip into a state of true laid-backness at this delightful and very tiny beachfront hideaway.

Four hexagonal, simply furnished but quite charming cottages are set in the trees at the edge of lovely White Bay beach, and ceiling fans capture the sea breezes. The two Beachfront Cottages have two rooms and the two Garden Cottages have one room. There are also two additional more traditionally shaped Garden Rooms with air-conditioning. This is the place to come when you want to read, relax, lie in a hammock, snorkel, snooze, make forays around the island, and come back for a quiet candlelit dinner. The location is at the busiest end of the beach, but it's kind of fun to see everyone come and go. The restaurant *(see page 41)* serves all meals and is excellent.

6 units. Daily rates: Beachfront Cottage $275 ($200), Garden Cottage $225 ($140), Garden Room $275 ($155) for two people not including taxes or meals. Closed Sept. Tel: 284.495.9888. Fax: 284.495.9999. www.sandcastle-bvi.com

JOST VAN DYKE COTTAGE AND HOUSE RENTALS
Note: Linens are provided but you will need to bring absolutely everything else, from salt to charcoal to paper towels, plus food. However, this is actually easy to do (the hardest part is making the perfect list). Whether you arrive from Tortola or St. Thomas (USVI), your taxi driver will stop at a grocery on the way to the ferry. (This is the best bet if you want to choose your vegetables, etc.) On Tortola, you may need to stop at several stores to find everything you need. You can also order in advance on line from www.amplehamper.com and have your provisions waiting at your villa. Suprettes on Jost Van Dyke do carry basics, but you never know which "basics" they will have at any given moment.

PINK HOUSE
Sleep to the sound of lapping waves in this charming and distinctive property just steps from a lovely white sand beach.

Tucked among palm trees at the eastern end of White Bay beach is this comfortable, pink-roofed West Indian-style house. It is about two dozen steps back from the water and is the only house at this end of the beach. On the main level are two simply furnished bedrooms, two bathrooms, a living room, a fully equipped kitchen, and a large porch. A third small room with a futon (most suitable for kids) is on the lower level. The large covered veranda looks out to views of White Bay and nearby islands. There is a charcoal grill, a stereo/CD player, a VCR and TV monitor (no TV reception), and a small collection of videos and books, and a washer/dryer. Rooms are cooled by ceiling fans. *Weekly rates: $3,900 ($2,900), more some holidays. Res: info@pinkhousebvi.com or 484.680.8150. www.pinkhousebvi.com*

SANDY GROUND ESTATES

Experience real isolation at these hillside houses on East End.

These eight one-, two-, and three-bedroom houses are tucked here and there in the hillside above a small but lovely beach with a good snorkeling reef at very remote East End. Each has been individually designed and each has a character all its own. One is perched on the rocks. Another is high on the hillside. Some are close to the beach. Houses are built some distance from each other and are extremely private. Many have outstanding views. All have full kitchens and VCRs with TV monitor (no TV reception) and ceiling fans. If you prefer not to bring supplies, management will stock the house. This complex is truly an escape and is very remote. It's a 20-minute walk to the nearest restaurant. However, with just a bit of a walk, you can get to a place where a taxi can pick you up for day or dinner trips to White Bay, Great Harbour, and Little Harbour. *8 villas. Weekly rates: $1,950 ($1,400) for two people, $300 ($200) for each additional person. Tel: 284.494.3391. Fax: 284.495.9379. www.sandyground.com*

WHITE BAY VILLAS

Enjoy dazzling views from these hillside cottages and houses that sit high above beautiful White Bay.

These units are built into the steep hillside above the east end of White Bay and the views of sea and neighboring islands are stunning. The three houses built out along the point of the hill are bright white with red tile roofs. The largest is a 4,000-square-foot multilevel house with two bedrooms, three baths, a large living/kitchen area and several verandas. Farther out on the point are an adjacent two-bedroom house and a one-bedroom house that can be combined as one rental. Set back into the hillside are three charming one-bedroom West Indian-style cottages. These cozy cottages have a separate living room and a deck. All units have kitchens with basic kitchen equipment and are cooled by ceiling fans. There are books, games, videos for the TV/VCR, and a stereo/CD player. A steep path leads down to the beach for morning swims and nighttime walks. *6 villas. Weekly rates: 3-bedroom villa $3,900 ($3,120), two-bedroom villa $2,900 ($2,320), one-bedroom villa and cottages $1,900 ($1,520). Res: Bonnie White at 410.571.6692. Fax: 410.571.6693. www.jostvandyke.com*

WHITE BAY CAMPGROUND

Ivan Chinnery, of Ivan's Stress-Free Bar fame, runs this simple campground with four equipped campsites (lamp and bed and ice chest inside a tent) for $35 a night; 10 bare campsites for $15 a night; and eight screened cabins with lamp, bed, and ice chest for $45 to $60 a night. Bathrooms and showers are near. *Tel: 284.495.9312 or 284.495.9358.*

FOXY CALLWOOD

How does a smiling, barefoot man from a tiny, out of the way island with only a hundred or so inhabitants become adored by people of all ages from all around the globe?

Radio? Television? Movies? The Internet?

Nope.

This man accomplished the impossible by teaming up with Tessa. By using his poetic and musical talent, his entrepreneurial genius, and, of course, that special smile. He accomplished the impossible by simply being himself.

Foxy didn't need movies, TV, or the Net to get to the people. He let the people come to him.

This wonderful, talented troubador from Jost Van Dyke has successful restaurants, bars, best-selling CDs, books written about him, beers named after him, beautiful women wanting to meet him and, yes, fish do fear him.

And for his fans it all started about 40 years ago with the first, modest Tamarind Bar. And Foxy smiles when he explains, "It was only supposed to be open for one day, for the Harvest Festival in 1967."

Well, 40 years later "Foxy's Wooden Boat Regatta," "Foxy's Halloween Party" and "Foxy's Old Year's Night Party" are famous the world over.

And so is Foxy, still barefoot and still smiling.

A DAY TRIP TO JOST VAN DYKE

This is an excellent one-day adventure that is just a 25-minute ferry ride from Tortola. Be sure to bring some cash (not every place takes credit cards), swimsuit, towel, sunscreen, camera, film, snorkel equipment. Bare feet are the norm at restaurants, but bring sturdy shoes if you want to hike the hills or the road.

The ferries leave from West End, Tortola (see schedules page 138). They double as delivery boats and when they are loaded, they often leave. Departure might be late, but it can also be early, so get to the dock with time to spare. You can pick up a soda across the street at Zelma's or a beer to go at Uncle Joe's Rocky Willow. Generally, the only indication that the boat is actually leaving is when someone begins to untie the lines. This is your cue to hop aboard. Sometimes you buy a ticket before boarding and sometimes you pay the $12 fare when you get to Jost Van Dyke (there is no ticket office).

After you leave the dock, the boat will pass Little Thatch and then turn right and clear passage between Great Thatch (on the left) and Tortola. Jost Van Dyke will be dead ahead and Tortola's north shore will appear on the right. Those two big green "gumdrops" of land on Tortola define Smuggler's Cove. Just beyond the farther "gumdrop" is Long Bay. You can't see Cane Garden Bay, but the distant hill with a long scar of erosion is at its far edge. Approaching Jost Van Dyke, you'll see two tiny islands on the right, each with a brilliant strip of white sand. The one closest to Jost Van Dyke is Green Cay. The other is Sandy Cay and is owned by Laurance Rockefeller. You can also see a strip of road that runs along Jost's hillside. This is the only road on the island.

The ferry takes you to the public dock on the west side of Great Harbour, the main "town" on Jost Van Dyke. White Bay and Little Harbour can be reached by taxi or a long walk.

WONDERFUL SIGHTS TO LOOK FOR

Goats in boats. If you think you've lost your mind because you think you see a dinghy full of animals out there, keep looking. It's probably goats. Islanders keep their goats on many of the uninhabited islands, and move them around on occasion, and it is not unusual to catch sight of a Boston Whaler with ten or twelve goats milling around!

Sea turtles. When you are snorkeling or floating or boating, look for big sea turtles. Before a turtle surfaces, it surreptitiously sticks its head out of the water to see what is going on. You can easily mistake it for a drifting stick.

Rays. You can sometimes spot a ray at rest when you are snorkeling over sand. Study the bottom carefully. They lie perfectly still and are almost indistinguishable from the sand.

Rainbows. Brilliant rainbows show up everywhere in the BVI, all day long. Even the briefest rain somewhere in the distance can create a rainbow and you'll get to see it splashed across the sky, radiant in the sunlight.

Double rainbows. The very luckiest people get to see complete double rainbows. Even a partial double is considered good luck.

Hummingbirds. They hang fluttering in the air close to flowering bushes, in glistening greens and blues.

VISITING ANOTHER ISLAND

No matter what island you are staying on, be sure to take at least one day trip to another British Virgin Island. These islands are remarkably different from one another. Each British Virgin Island has its own unique personality.

It's very easy to get from one island to another by public ferry. You can catch a return ferry in the late afternoon, and from some islands, you can also stay for dinner and head home after dark — a nighttime boat ride under a sky full of brilliant stars with the island lights twinkling in the distance is hard to beat!

If you are staying on Tortola you can catch a ferry to Anegada, Cooper, Jost Van Dyke, Marina Cay, Peter Island, Virgin Gorda (North Sound and The Valley), and St. John and St. Thomas in the USVI. From Virgin Gorda, you can take a ferry to Anegada, Saba Rock, Tortola (West End, Road Town, and East End/Beef Island), and St. Thomas in the USVI. If you are staying on Jost Van Dyke you can take a ferry to West End, Tortola and to St. John and St. Thomas in the USVI. From Anegada, you can take a ferry to Tortola and The Valley in Virgin Gorda. If you are staying on Cooper Island, you can take a ferry to a dock near Road Town, Tortola. From Marina Cay, you can take a ferry to East End/Beef Island, Tortola. If you are staying on Peter Island, you can take a ferry to a dock near Road Town, Tortola.

You can also join an organized day trip to various islands, charter a boat, or rent a little powerboat (see boat trip/rental sections in the chapters on Jost Van Dyke, Tortola, and Virgin Gorda; see water taxis page 36). No matter how you decide to go, don't miss the chance to visit another island.

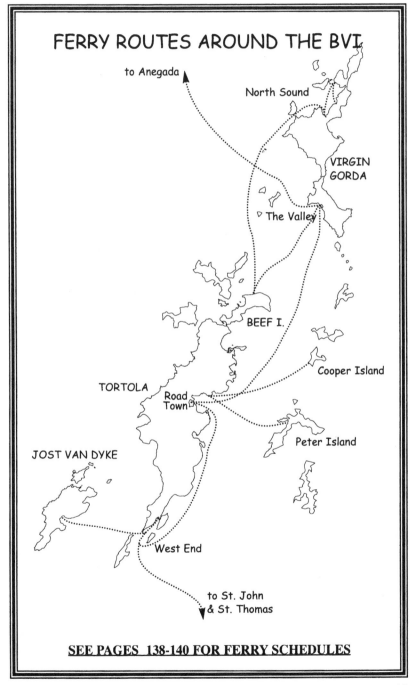

FERRY ROUTES AROUND THE BVI

to Anegada

North Sound

VIRGIN GORDA

The Valley

BEEF I.

Cooper Island

TORTOLA

Road Town

Peter Island

JOST VAN DYKE

West End

to St. John & St. Thomas

SEE PAGES 138-140 FOR FERRY SCHEDULES

THE NICEST MAN IN THE WORLD

Jost Van Dyke's Ivan Chinnery is the owner and proprietor of **Ivan's Local Flavor Stress Free Bar** and **White Bay Campground** and the creator and often the star of **The International All Stars Ever Changing Band**.

Ivan represents the best of the BVI. In fact, he may be the human manifestation of what these unique islands are all about.

He is smooth. He is laid back. He is interested, interesting, kind, friendly, trusting. He is genuine.

If you were choosing teams, Ivan is the kind of person you would choose first for your team—even if he weren't the best player.

Everybody loves Ivan. Sure Mick Jagger and Keith Richards and Kenny Chesney are fans, but it's not just celebrities. Locals, ex-pats, and savvy tourists flock to Ivan's when it's time to chill out, when it is time for stress-free rest, when it's time for a measure of Ivan's contagious good humor.

And if you ask anyone who has met Ivan, if you even mention his name in a conversation and someone next to you hears it, the response is almost always the same, almost always something like: "Ivan, yeah, isn't he the nicest man in the world!"

7. MARINA CAY

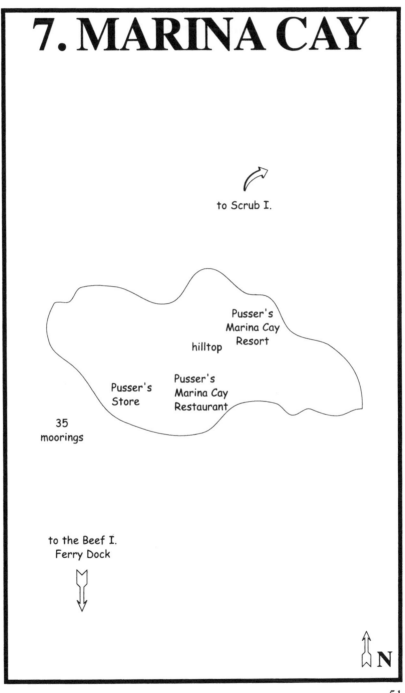

to Scrub I.

Pusser's
Marina Cay
Resort

hilltop

Pusser's
Store

Pusser's
Marina Cay
Restaurant

35
moorings

to the Beef I.
Ferry Dock

N

MARINA CAY

This tiny bit of rock that pokes its head out of the water between Beef Island and Great Camanoe is hardly big enough to be called an island. Indeed, it covers just eight acres! It's a great anchorage and there are 35 moorings here; it's the site of the Pusser's Marina Cay Resort, Pusser's Marina Cay Restaurant, and a Pusser's Company Store.

WHAT YOU CAN DO ON MARINA CAY

You can dine or have a drink at the restaurant and shop in Pusser's. You can also sun yourself on the little beach, swim in calm water, and enjoy great snorkeling over the shallow reef that extends out from much of this islet. It's possible to walk completely around Marina Cay in a relatively short amount of time provided you have shoes to protect your feet from the rocks and the sharp coral. There's a second little beach past the docks and a bunch of rocks.

HOW TO GET THERE

There are free ferries from Beef Island at the ferry dock on Trellis Bay. *(See page 140 for schedules.)*

Pusser's Marina Cay Restaurant *(284 494.2174)* sits along the edge of the beach and is open for lunch and dinner (and breakfast for hotel guests). Appetizers include conch fritters and deep-fried calamari. At lunch you can get hot dogs, burgers, burritos, and various salads. The dinner menu includes ribs, steak, lobster, fish, and pasta. *LD $$*

Pusser's Company Store *(284.494.2174)* is built out over the water and features the Pusser's line of casual clothing for the whole family, plus books, nautical memorabilia, swimwear, postcards, and much more.

Pusser's Marina Cay Resort units are on the opposite side of the hillside from the restaurant and look out over the water. Four rooms each have a king-size bed, a little refrigerator, ceiling fans (no air-conditioning, but it's almost always very breezy here), and balcony. There are also two two-bedroom suites. Continental breakfast is included in the rates. Guests can rent hobie cats or ocean kayaks or head across to Trellis Bay to windsurf. And, of course, they can take the ferry to Beef Island and explore Tortola for the day.
6 units. *Rates: $225 a night for two ($155 off season); suites $485 ($330 off season). Tel: 284.494.2174. Fax: 284.494.4775. www.pussers.com*

ANGUILLA (OR ST. BART'S) FOR THE DAY

You're already in the Caribbean. Why not have a great adventure and go down island for the day?

Anguilla is just 87 miles to the east of Virgin Gorda. It's the "next" island down in the leeward chain. Anguilla is a flat island with gorgeous beaches, great restaurants, some very fancy hotels, and a gorgeous 18-hole golf course, but it's also a quiet and immensely friendly island.

The Flight
The plane leaves from Virgin Gorda at 8:30 am and departs from Anguilla around 4 pm (or you can be picked up at and returned to Tortola/Beef Island). You'll fly over Sombrero, a little island halfway between Virgin Gorda and Anguilla. On the way back, the pilot will fly you over the Baths for a great bird's-eye view of these giant boulders and stunning blue water.

On Anguilla
A tour guide will meet you and take you on a tour around Anguilla, stopping by the well-known Cap Juluca Hotel, the Malliouhana Hotel, and beautiful beaches. Or you can be taken to your destination of choice. Or you can spend the day playing golf at Anguilla's beautiful 18-hole Temenos Golf Course.

The Details
The plane is a 10-seater, the flight is 40 minutes, and the fee is $260 per person, minimum of six. (Fewer people can go, but the price can't go lower than for six.) A similar trip is available to St. Bart's. Ask for details. Call Derrick Gumbs *(284.495.5346 or 284.499.1552)*, call the Anguilla office *(264.497.8690)* or e-mail derrick_transanguillaairway@hotmail.com. Have fun and don't forget your passport!

CHARTERING A SAILBOAT

The British Virgin Islands are one of the most popular chartering areas in the world. If you have ever dreamed about a boating vacation, this is the place to come. You can be your own captain, or hire one.

The BVI nautical environment is almost perfect for charterers. The trade winds blow steadily and the waters are relatively calm. There are a zillion wonderful anchorages, many off deserted islands. There are also many, many anchorages with moorings, so you can just sail in and pick one up, rather than worry all night about whether your anchor is dragging. In addition, because the islands are so close together, line of sight navigation is almost always possible and, if it gets a bit too windy or rough wherever you are, there is almost always a nearby bay facing a different direction to slip into for shelter.

Because the BVI is so popular with charterers, there are many islands with beach bars just awaiting your arrival. You won't want to miss stopping at the Cooper Island Beach Club, Norman Island (where you'll find great snorkeling and a beach bar and restaurant and the floating Willy T's), Cane Garden Bay, and, of course, famous Foxy's on Jost Van Dyke.

The Moorings is the world's largest chartering operation and they have a huge fleet of boats at their Road Town base. Catamarans and 51' yachts are the most popular choices and you can bareboat or decide to go with a captain. *(Tel: 888.952.8420, 284.494.2331. www.moorings.com)*. Another reliable outfit is **Barecat Charters** at Soper's Hole. This company specializes in catamarans, which many prefer to charter because of the comfort and stability of the craft. *(Tel: 800.296.5287, 284.495.1979. www.barecat.com)*.

8. NECKER

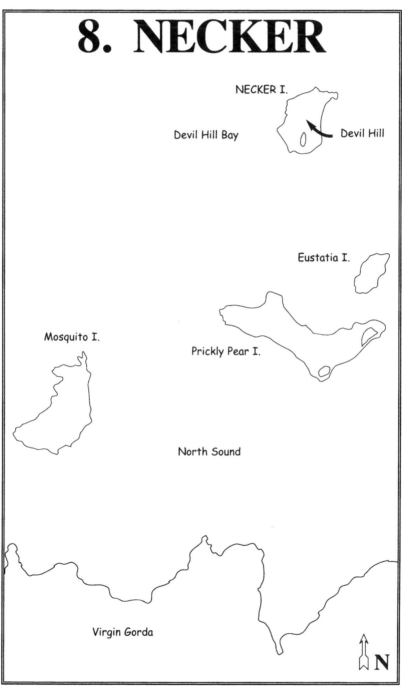

NECKER I.

Devil Hill Bay

Devil Hill

Eustatia I.

Mosquito I.

Prickly Pear I.

North Sound

Virgin Gorda

N

NECKER

Necker is a luxurious, 74-acre private island surrounded by coral reefs that sits just north of Virgin Gorda and you rent the whole thing. This is the place to come if you want a lot of privacy and plenty of pampering. Mel Gibson, Harrison Ford, Oprah Winfrey, and Steven Spielberg are just some of the many famous guests who have rented here. You can swim at empty beaches, dine on gourmet food, and walk along winding paths through brilliant tropical flowers. At stops on every walk are baskets full of sodas, wine, and cold champagne, just in case that's what you were thinking of having.

For two separate weeks during the year, one can experience Necker without reserving the entire island. During these Celebration Weeks, up to 13 couples (who probably don't know each other) arrive to a kind of "house-party" setting, with their own private bedroom and bath, but sharing the living quarters and dining together.

Necker Island is a truly luxurious tropical paradise. White sand beaches ring the shoreline and brilliant tropical flowers seem to be everywhere. Perched on a hill is a Balinese villa with a sort of giant, high-ceilinged, indoor-outdoor living room open to soft breezes. Bedroom doors fold back completely, providing awesome views right from your pillow. Three Balinese villas have additional bedrooms. Resident chefs work magic in the state-of-the-art kitchen and a staff of 24 await your requests. Paths lead through the manicured grounds to beaches, swimming pools, tennis court, a 300-year-old Hindu meditation hut, and hidden hammocks.
Daily rates: $37,500 1-14 people, additional $1,250 per guest to 20 people. Celebration Weeks: $22,500 per couple for the week. Rates include almost everything. Res: 800.557.4255. www.neckerisland.com

---

SEAGRAPE COTTAGE ON LITTLE THATCH

If you want something a bit smaller than Necker, head to this breezy West Indian beachfront cottage with kitchen on a 55-acre private island just west of Tortola and perfect for honeymooners. The island's owners visit their hilltop villa but much of the time the island will feel like it's all yours, although charterboats do anchor here during the day. *Weekly rates for two people: $8,950 ($5,775 off season) plus provisioning, if requested. Tel: 284.495.9227. Fax: 284.495.9212.*

RAINY DAYS

Rainy days are rare in the British Virgin Islands but if it happens to rain on one of the days you are in the BVI, here are some great things to do.

❖ Schedule a massage or a yoga class
at Fort Recovery.

❖ Find someone you love and take a
long rainy walk on the beach.

❖ Get a book and read quietly where you can
see and hear the rain and
smell the tropical moisture
but still keep dry
(in light rains a palm tree is fine shelter).

❖ Write and send a dozen postcards to people you
like, or to people you don't like.

❖ Go for a swim in a pool.

❖ Play a board game, like Parcheesi or Clue.
Most places have these games around
and they're still fun, whether you are 12 or 112.

❖ Take photographs—rain showers, rainbows, slick
palm fronds, patterns of rain on water.

❖ Sit, listen, and watch...spend time just pausing.

SCUBA DIVING

Many people have no idea that dive outfits in the BVI offer simple Resort Courses where qualified instructors teach you how to scuba dive in just a few hours, in the safety of a quiet pool, and then take you out for a real dive over a reef or a wreck. You go down 40 to 50 feet with trained instructors by your side.

Many who have tried this go on to become certified divers. Almost everybody says that it is an amazing and wonderful experience, and some say it is even easier than snorkeling.

For experienced divers, the BVI offer some exceptionally interesting shipwrecks, including the 2,434-ton *H.M.S. Rhone*, plus caves, reefs, walls, pinnacles, ledges, and archways, all in unusually clear water. Night dives, which show off amazing things you can't see underwater during the day, are popular here, too.

On Tortola, call **Blue Water Divers** *at Nanny Cay (284.494.2847) or* **Dive Tortola** *at Prospect Reef Marina near Road Town (284.494.9200).*

On Virgin Gorda **DIVE BVI** *works out of Leverick Bay (284.495.7328) and the Virgin Gorda Yacht Harbour (284.495.5513) and also at Marina Cay.* **Kilbride's Underwater Tours** *is at the Bitter End Yacht Club on Virgin Gorda's North Sound (284.495.9638).*

"We want to explore the themes of the ocean's existence . . . how it harmonizes the physical and biological rhythms of the whole earth."
— Jacques Cousteau

9. PETER

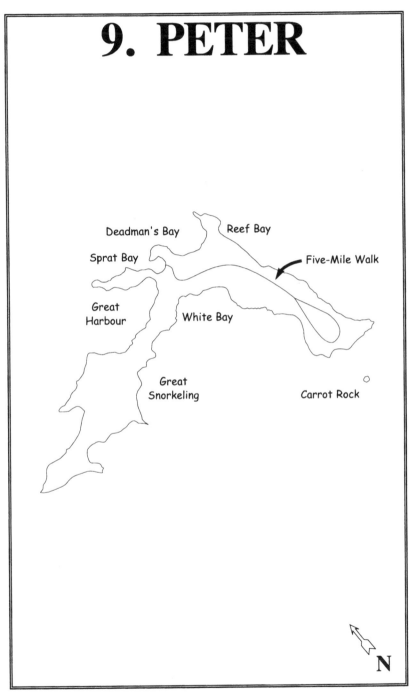

Deadman's Bay

Reef Bay

Sprat Bay

Five-Mile Walk

Great
Harbour

White Bay

Great
Snorkeling

Carrot Rock

N

PETER

Peter Island is a lush and mountainous private island five miles south of Tortola. The Peter Island Resort and Yacht Harbour is nestled along the north shore and there are five beautiful beaches. What magazine articles and books omit about this resort is that the resort facilities only take up a tiny bit of this four-and-a-half-mile-long island. The rest of the island is undeveloped, except for the Eagle's Nest, a private residence that sits atop the island's highest point. Although there are no cars on the island, several roads lead through this hilly woodland and there are marvelous opportunities for long, scenic walks, including the famous five-mile walk that starts from Sprat Bay. Several bays on Peter Island are popular anchorages and there are moorings on Sprat Bay. The ferry schedule (see page 140) makes it easy to come from Road Town for lunch or dinner.

Peter Island Resort and Yacht Harbour has just 52 rooms, 32 on a spit of land looking out over the Sir Francis Drake Channel, and another 20 clustered at one end of Deadman's Bay. The junior "suites," located on a low bluff at the western edge of Deadman's Bay, are comfortable rooms with a cozy sitting area facing the bed, and with romantic bathtubs that open onto tropical greenery. There are four to a building, two upstairs and two downstairs. The lower units open onto grassy areas and stairs that lead to the beach and the upper units have higher ceilings, a bit more privacy, and more dramatic views. The rooms near the dock are smaller and are also four to a building. The first floor Garden View rooms look out across the pool or into the gardens and have a little sitting alcove. The slightly smaller second-floor Ocean View rooms with higher A-frame ceilings look across the pool and gardens to the water. There are five beaches, a water sports program, a disappearing-edge swimming pool, tennis courts, a fitness trail, an exercise room, and a full-service spa that overlooks the beach, with a plunge pool and a complete menu of treatments.

The **Tradewinds Restaurant** is the resort's signature restaurant and it is air-conditioned but can be opened to the island breezes. Breakfast is served here daily. Dinner is a la carte and there is a different, and extensive, menu every night but Saturday, when there is a Grand Buffet. There is live entertainment several evenings a week on season. **Deadman's Bay Bar and Grill** is open every day for lunch and offers both a buffet and an a la carte menu. Dinner is served here several nights a week.

52 units, 5 private villas. Rates including all meals: $900-$1,425 ($560-$965 off season) plus 17% tax and service charge. Res: 800.346.4451. Tel: 284.495.2000. Fax: 284.495.2500. www.peterisland.com

AMAZING NIGHTS IN THE BVI

★Anchoring in Cane Garden Bay and hearing
the melodic sounds of local recording star
Quito Rymer
drift across the water—beautiful ballads
and love songs accompanied by sweet guitar.

★Any beach on a moonless night,
when the sky is ablaze with about ten times more stars
than you have ever seen before.

★Bomba's Full-Moon Parties on Tortola,
when there seem to be more people
than you thought live in the entire BVI.

★Foxy's much-loved and very famous
New Year's Eve extravaganzas
on Jost Van Dyke—when there are
so many boats at anchor
that you can practically hop
from boat to boat all the way to shore.

★Dancing cheek-to-cheek under the stars
at elegant Biras Creek or Little Dix Bay.

★Walking a deserted beach
under a brilliant full moon, when it's so bright
that the possibility of "moon-burn"
occurs to you for the very first time.

GREAT THINGS TO DO

Walk on a beach at night - take in the sounds and sights, the stars, the moon, and look for the magic of the sparkling phosphorescence at the water's edge.

Experience a sunrise along a beach - you don't have to do it the morning after your night beach walk, and you don't have to stay up all night. Just get up a little early (you can always go back to bed).

Do a drive - pick one of the drives in this book or make one up, but do get up into the hills of Tortola or Virgin Gorda for some truly magnificent views.

Go somewhere in a boat - go anywhere or nowhere.

Spend an hour alone doing nothing - inside or out, day or night - no TV, no iPod, no writing, no reading, just you and yourself for an hour doing absolutely nothing.

Catch the BBC news from London - it's on radio ZBVI.

Take a day trip to another island - go to Jost or Anegada or Tortola or an uninhabited cay.

Go to a horse race - they're held once a month at the track at Sea Cow's Bay, and they're a lot of fun!

See the islands from the air - call Fly BVI *(284.495.1747)* or Island Helicopters *(284.499.263, 284.496.8477)* and take a flightseeing trip to catch the spectacular views from above!

Float - just lie on one of those wonderful floats in the warm Caribbean Sea and do nothing, just float.

10. TORTOLA

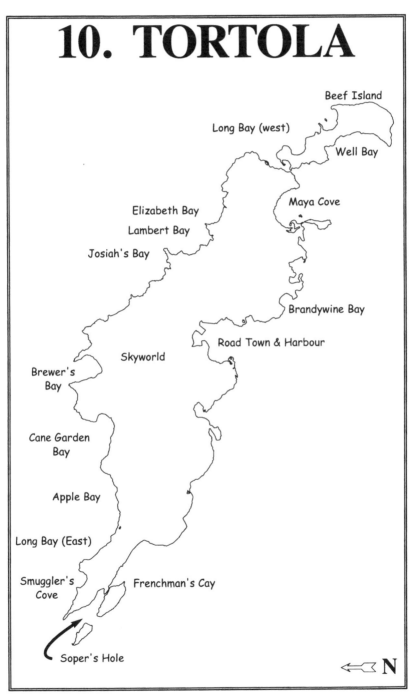

Beef Island

Long Bay (west)

Well Bay

Maya Cove

Elizabeth Bay

Lambert Bay

Josiah's Bay

Brandywine Bay

Skyworld

Road Town & Harbour

Brewer's Bay

Cane Garden Bay

Apple Bay

Long Bay (East)

Smuggler's Cove

Frenchman's Cay

Soper's Hole

N

TORTOLA IN A NUTSHELL

Tortola is the largest British Virgin Island and exceptionally hilly. There is virtually no flat land. Houses are scattered on the steep hillsides and roads hug the shoreline or run feverishly up and down the island's multiple peaks showing off stunning, airplane-like views.

This island is by far the most populated British Virgin Island, with over 19,000 people (or over 80% of the entire BVI population). Nestled against Tortola's south shore is Road Town, the capital of the BVI.

Road Town, which is built almost entirely on reclaimed land, is the only real town in the entire country. Government buildings, plus grocery, plumbing, office supply, and hardware stores are mixed in with bars, restaurants, shops, and marinas. There's also a cruise ship dock, public ferry dock, and Customs Office. The town can be trafficky and dusty (or muddy if its been raining) and parking can be difficult.

At the west end of the island is tiny West End, where there is a public ferry dock and Customs Office; the little harbor known as Sopher's Hole; and, a five-minute drive around the harbor, Frenchman's Cay, which is home to a marina, and a little cluster of shops, restaurants, and two grocery stores. The east end of the island, including Beef Island (which is only 600 feet from Tortola and the location of the airport), is even less developed but has a few excellent restaurants and several art galleries.

Most of Tortola's resorts (see page 99) are located on the western part of the island but villa rentals are scattered all over and can also be found on Beef Island (where the airport is). Most of the best beaches, some with little restaurants and bars, some completely undeveloped, are strung along Tortola's entire north shore.

WHAT YOU CAN DO ON TORTOLA

Swim, snorkel, hike, horseback ride, see stunning views, walk along exceptionally beautiful beaches, drive remarkably hilly roads, eat outside almost all the time day and night—whether you're at a local "fish fry"or a fancy gourmet restaurant, drink barefoot at beachside bars, rent a boat, take a boat ride . . . the list goes on and on. Shopping is on a small scale but there are great things to buy if you know where on the island to look.

64

EXPLORING TORTOLA

Spectacular panoramic vistas are one of Tortola's most outstanding features. Although the roads are remarkably steep in places, many people will want to rent a car and drive, at least once, to catch these stunning views. If you are truly faint of heart, then opt for a taxi tour.

TORTOLA'S AMAZING ROADS

On Tortola, there's almost no such thing as a straight, flat piece of road. This mountainous island isn't a single steep mound, but rather a collection of many, many knobby hilltops. Tortola's road system is draped over these knobs, dropping swiftly to sea level every once in a while to skirt a shimmering bay or run along a crescent of beach.

The roads themselves are astonishing: a collection of hairpin turns and dizzying descents and ascents that often are bordered by precipitous drops. Because of this, Tortola's scenery is especially spectacular from a car. When you are driving on this island you are constantly changing altitude and frequently looking across plummeting valleys to other hilltops, with sweeping views of the sea and other islands beyond. There are many views from over 1,000 feet.

Renting a jeep or a car. In Road Town, delightful Ms. Burke at **ITGO** *(284.494.5150, www.itgobvi.com, free pickup at all hotels)* at the Mill Mall complex is the person to see. **Hertz** has offices at West End *(284.495.4405)*, Road Town *(284.494.6228)*, and the airport *(284.495.6600)*. **Dollar Rent A Car** has offices at Long Bay Resort *(284.495.4772)*. **National** has offices at Long Bay Resort *(284.495.4877)*. Jeeps run $50-60 a day, less off season. The rental agency will provide you with a temporary BVI license ($10 plus a valid license from home). Remember, driving is on the left.

Taxis and taxi tours. Almost any taxi will take you around the island for about $50. Hilroy Douglas *(284.494.4064, 284.499.3975)* is a good choice for a tour or if you need to be picked up at a certain time to catch a plane. For a taxi in West End, call 284.495.4934 or 284.495.4881; in Road Town call 284.494.6362 or 284.494.4959 (Atlee Chawell and Alfred Freeman are great); in East End call 284.495.1982 or Godfrey Gumbs at 284.499.2947 or 284.499.3604. Expect to share taxis with fellow travelers. Fares range from $3 per person for a short ride (such as from one part of Road Town to another) to $12 per person from West End to Road Town to $18 per person from one end of Tortola to the other. Even if you rent a car, it can be more relaxing to take a taxi to a distant restaurant.

HINTS FOR DRIVING ON TORTOLA

❑On steep hills, in automatic cars, if you can't get enough power, even in low gear, turn off the air-conditioning and you'll be okay.

❑Driving is on the left. This is the trickiest when you are turning from one road onto another or heading into a roundabout. Invent a reminder, like staying on the same side of the road as your heart.

❑Share the driving. Managing the roads requires constant attention, so the driver misses the views.

❑Try to keep track, on a map, of where you think you are so you'll recognize a turn. There are few road signs and the twists and turns happen fast.

❑Hills and curves look completely different from the other direction, so a road you have just driven can look totally unfamiliar on the return trip. Don't feel stupid. You're not lost.

❑Beware those tight little curves you see on a map—those are hills! However, distances are short, and almost everything is only 10 minutes away from the last thing, even if it is over switchbacks.

❑Tailgaters are common, and can hang unnervingly close behind you. If they annoy you, pull to the side and let them pass. When you tire of doing this, just stop looking in the rearview mirror.

❑Speaking of mirrors, keep a lookout for mirrors on hills and curves. These are specially positioned to give you a view of oncoming traffic that you can't otherwise see.

❑When you encounter goats or cows being herded along the road, just slow down and politely make your way through. Watch also for the stray goat, or cow, or horse that is standing in the road intently munching on the leaves of an overhanging tree branch.

❑Do be very careful. "Island time" doesn't seem to apply to driving here and you'll encounter Indianapolis 500 wannabes.

A SPECTACULAR TEN-MINUTE DRIVE

FROM ROAD TOWN TO SKYWORLD

This drive takes you on an ear-popping 1,300-foot ascent in about eight breathtaking minutes. It's an awesome trip in both directions. At the top is an observation deck with the highest 360-degree view in the BVI. It's possible to see Anegada and even St. Croix, which is 40 miles away. There's also a great restaurant, Skyworld, and a neat little shop.

Time: 10 minutes each way, plus however long you stay mesmerized by the view at Skyworld.
When to do this: On clear days you can see the farthest. Sunsets here are gorgeous.

From the ferry dock in Road Town, head east (keeping the water on your right) along Waterfront Drive toward the center of Road Town. Stay on this road several minutes, until you come to a roundabout. Bear left, into the roundabout, and take your very first left out of the roundabout, by the Shell station. You'll quickly come to a "T" in the road. Turn right onto Main Street (keeping, of course, to the left side of the road). Take your first real left, which will head uphill. Sometimes this road sign says Joe's Hill Road, sometimes it says Cane Garden Bay, and sometimes it's not there. Soon after you've turned, those on the right side of the car can start looking down at some great views of Road Town and Road Harbour.

After some sharp twists back and forth, there is an extremely severe switchback curve that climbs up at an almost impossible angle. (Your ears should have popped by now.) The switchback spits you out onto an almost level bit of road just as you pass a white two-story building on your left. Bear right and keep on going. You'll start heading up again.

Soon you'll see a spectacular view of neighboring islands on the left. There are several little pull-off areas on your left where you can stop to look at the views and take photographs.

Watch carefully for the sign to Skyworld. The sign is on the left but the turn is actually to the right, and it's an extremely sharp right turn that also heads

67

up. After you turn right, you'll pass an elementary school (imagine going to school every day and having these views out your window!) and then you'll be on a narrow ridge with a pasture sweeping down to your left. Just ahead is a hill.

Now is the time to look for the entrance to Skyworld. The sign isn't always there but it's your first left and it is steep. Drive straight up until you are spilled out onto a little plateau with a parking lot. Pull in, get out, and enjoy the view.

From here, looking south, you can see the entire chain of islands that border the Sir Francis Drake Channel. From left to right, they are the south end of Virgin Gorda, Fallen Jerusalem, Round Rock (the little one), Ginger, Cooper, Salt, Peter, Norman, and tiny Pelican Island. The small island farthest to the right is the easternmost USVI, which is called Flanagan Island.

For a lunch or beverage with a great view, head to the entrance of the building, which is the Skyworld Restaurant. To reach the observation deck, follow the path just to the right of the restaurant entrance, which leads around to a set of stairs. There is a gift shop there, too.

RETURNING FROM SKYWORLD
Retracing your steps is easy except for one place. After you've turned right out of the Skyworld driveway, and turned left after the school, you'll be on level road for a while. Watch for the white two-story house and take the abrupt left just before the house. Be prepared for some truly spectacular airplane-like views as you drop about 1100 feet in the four or five minutes it takes to get back to sea level. To get back to the roundabout when you reach the bottom of this amazing hill, go left and then take your first right. Follow it to the end, turn left, and you'll be back in the roundabout.

"Be prepared for some truly spectacular
airplane-like views as you drop about 1100 feet
in the four or five minutes it takes
to get back to sea level."

TORTOLA'S GREAT BEACHES

Tortola's best beaches are tucked along the island's north shore. It's here that you will find picture-perfect crescents of glistening white sand bordered by sea grapes and palm trees. Some are very easy to reach. Others have bumpy and steep approaches. You may be the only one on the beach and there are no lifeguards so be careful when swimming.

Long Bay Beach (East) is actually on Beef Island and is long and lovely and good for swimming. Head toward the airport but turn left just past the salt flats and then follow the dirt road which curves to the right around the flats (and please don't drive across the flats).

Lambert Beach, on the eastern end of Tortola's north shore, is a good swimming beach unless the surf is up. Then watch out for strong undertows. You can use the pool at the Lambert Beach Resort for a fee.

Josiah's Bay Beach is often completely deserted. Some days this east end beach can have strong undertows. Follow Little Dick's Road from the Long Look Police Station and go right at the sign (before the hill). There are two simple snack bars for burgers and beers.

Brewer's Bay is a long and bumpy ride down but worth the discomfort. It's a calm beach great for swimming and snorkeling and there are old Sugar Mill Ruins. The easier access from Ridge Road is just past (if you are driving west) the green garbage bin and white house. A restaurant and bar is at the west end of the beach.

Cane Garden Bay is the closest beach to Road Town (15 minutes) even though it's on the north shore. Because it is so accessible and so famous, it can just be too crowded at times. Definitely skip it when cruise ships are in Road Town. It's too picturesque to miss completely, so try stopping by in the early morning or evening or anytime off season. From Road Town, just follow the directions to Skyworld *(page 67)* but go straight instead of right when you see the first Skyworld sign and follow the road down to sea level.

Apple Bay, home of the famous Bomba's Shack, is a narrow strip of beach that is the most popular surfing beach on Tortola because of the rollers coming in from the Atlantic.

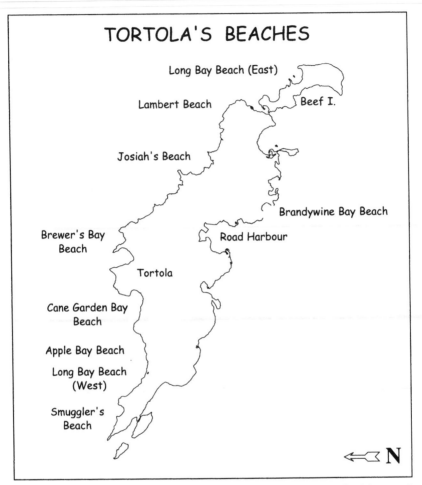

TORTOLA'S BEACHES

Long Bay Beach (East)

Lambert Beach

Beef I.

Josiah's Beach

Brandywine Bay Beach

Brewer's Bay Beach

Road Harbour

Tortola

Cane Garden Bay Beach

Apple Bay Beach

Long Bay Beach (West)

Smuggler's Beach

N

Long Bay Beach (West) is a stunning mile-long stretch of white sand that is never crowded. Long Bay Beach Resort, which fronts part of it, has a nice beach restaurant and bar.

Smuggler's Cove takes a bit of bouncing around to get to but it's one of Tortola's most picture-perfect beaches. A wide crescent of white sand wraps along most of the shore and the water is the color of turquoise neon light. This bay is almost always calm and on some days can be as still as a pond. The bottom is sandy and deepens very gradually. *(See page 77 for a more complete description.)*

Brandywine Bay beach (east of Road Town) is small with calm waters.

THINGS THAT ARE FUN TO DO ON TORTOLA

❏For truly breathtaking views, drive the entire length of Ridge Road, which zigs and zags along Tortola's many mountaintops. Don't miss the historical Great Wall at Fahie Hill on Ridge Road, a series of murals by local artists that depict life as it used to be in the BVI.

❏Visit the J. R. O'Neal Botanic Gardens in Road Town. They're open daily from 8 am to 6 pm and you'll see all kinds of exotic flowers and plants, including medicinal plants.

❏Go to a local sporting event. Check the local papers to see what is going on during your stay. There can be softball games, rugby matches, horse races, and sailing regattas.

❏Head to the docks and watch boats come and go. It's fun to watch the skilled skippers navigate so effortlessly, and even more fun to watch some of the less-experienced charterers try to manage. In Road Town, go to Village Cay Marina or the Moorings. At West End, go to Pusser's on Frenchman's Cay.

❏Drive or take a taxi to the observation platform at Skyworld. It is less than 10 minutes from Road Town and the views are unmatchable. Bring your camera and just keep shooting. This is the highest unobstructed 360-degree view in the BVI. On a clear day you can even see Anegada.

❏Go horseback riding. Shadow *(284.494.2262)* offers great guided horseback-riding trips up into Tortola's hills and down along the island's beaches.

GREAT WATER SPORTS

Cane Garden Bay on Tortola and Trellis Bay on Beef Island are two very protected bays and are the two most popular areas for windsurfing, kayaking, and sunfishing. You can also go waterskiing on Cane Garden Bay. On calm days it is wonderful fun to rent your own little powerboat and go wherever you want.

WINDSURFING, WATERSKIING, AND KAYAKING

Cane Garden Bay Pleasure Boats *(284.495.9660)* rents Hobie Cats, sailboats, sunfish, windsurfers, kayaks, canoes, and snorkel equipment. Prices range from $20 an hour for a sunfish to $30 an hour for a Hobie Cat. You can go water-skiing for about $50 a half hour or $75 an hour.

Boardsailing BVI *(284.495.2447)* at Trellis Bay on Beef Island rents equipment by the hour, day, and week, and offers all levels of instruction.

RENTING LITTLE POWERBOATS

Cane Garden Bay Pleasure Boats *(284.495.9660)* rents 18'-24' powerboats with a bimini, cooler, and ship-to-shore radio for $200-$350 a day, including fuel. **Island Time** *(284.495.9993)*, at Village Cay, rents 22' 150 hp powerboats with a bimini for $250 a day, plus fuel. **Sheppard Powerboat Rentals** *(284.495.4099)* operates out of his own marina at Soper's Hole and rents Mako 25' power boats with a center console and bimini for $375 per day plus fuel. A captain is $100 additional per day. **Sunshine Pleasure Boats** *(284.494.8813)* located at Village Cay Marina in Road Town offers powerboats for rent. Call for rates.

HAVE LUNCH OR DINNER ON ANOTHER ISLAND!

If you are staying on Tortola and want to have dinner on Virgin Gorda (or vise versa), call **Speedy's** *(284.495.5235, 284.495.5240)*, which has a ferry leaving for Virgin Gorda at 6:45 pm and returning at 10:30 pm and leaving Virgin Gorda at 6 pm and returning at 11 pm. *(See page 138 for daytime schedules.)* If you want to go to Cooper or Jost Van Dyke or any other island for dinner (or for the day), or if you just need transportation to another island and want to take a water taxi, then call **Sheppard Power Boat Rentals and Water Taxis** *(284.495.4099)*.

GREAT SNORKEL TRIPS AND BOAT TRIPS TO OTHER ISLANDS

Remarkably, from Tortola, it's only three to five miles to all the other British Virgin Islands, except far-flung Anegada, and there are excellent boat trips available to all the islands, even Anegada. For a very reasonable price you can go with a group or charter a small boat with a captain. These trips leave from Road Town or Soper's Hole at West End. Almost all take most major credit cards. Many boat trips head to other islands and to several great snorkeling spots. Exactly where they go will depend on the weather that day, and especially on how windy it is. Some of these trips stop at a restaurant on an island and others serve lunch on board.

If you know how to handle boats and prefer to be in charge, you can also rent a little powerboat and take yourself on your own snorkel trip or off to visit another island (see page 72). It's best to do this when the weather is calm.

What to bring? Towel and bathing suit, sunscreen, your own snorkel gear if you have a prescription mask, camera, and film.

Aristocat Charters *(284.499.1249, 284.495.4087,www.aristocatcharters.com)* offers half-day, full-day, and sunset cruises on a spacious, stable 48' catamaran. Lunch, beverages, and snorkel gear are provided. The boat sails from Soper's Hole in West End and destinations can include Jost Van Dyke, Norman, and Peter Islands. Rates are $100 per person for a full day.

Kuralu *(284.495.4381, www.kuralu.com)* is a 50' luxury cruising catamaran that is so popular it's booked almost every day. Robin Pinfold is the owner and captain, and his charming golden retriever is often first mate! This is a fine trip for families and children as there is safety netting around the boat. Choose from two trips. One goes to Green Cay for snorkeling and then makes a great spinnaker sail to Jost Van Dyke. After lunch on board, you can swim or snorkel and stop at Foxy's before the return sail. The other trip goes to the Indians for snorkeling and to Benures Bay where you can swim with big turtles. Lunch is usually several salads, quiche, a variety of cheeses and cold meats, and French bread. Since Robin is usually out every day, just leave a message on his machine saying where and when you want to go, the number of people, and where you are staying. He'll be sure to get back to you that evening. Trips are around $100 per person (around $50 for children under 12).

Mystique (284.494.0740, www.voyagecharters.com) is a 45' catamaran that sails daily out of Soper's Hole, but don't worry about getting to the boat. They'll get you there and back and the land transportation is included in the rate. *Mystique* has a seat for everyone in the covered cockpit and more than enough room outside for the sun worshippers. Take your choice. There are also hot showers and private changing rooms aboard. Three different day-sail itineraries are offered: Sandy Cay, White Bay, and Norman Island. Trips are $90 or $100 and include all your drinks on board.

Patouche Charters *(284.494.6300, www.patouche.com)* offers snorkeling trips to nearby islands via catamaran and includes guided underwater tours and snorkel instruction. These are good trips for people who have never snorkeled, but seasoned snorkelers will also enjoy them because of the destinations. Choose between a half day and one or two snorkel stops or a full day and two or three snorkel stops plus lunch. In either case, you'll be with 6 to 16 other people. They usually go snorkeling near Norman, Cooper, and Peter. Rates per person are $60 half day (one-two snorkel sites) and $100 for a full day (two-three snorkel sites and lunch). They have several boats, including the *Sandy Cay*, a Bertram that used to be part of the Little Dix fleet. Private charters are available on any of their boats and they will customize a trip just for you!

Silmaril (284.495.9225, www.peterisland.com/silmaril.html) is a 41' sailing yacht based at Peter Island. Paul and Judy will come pick you up anywhere on the south side of Tortola for a day (or half day) of whatever you want to do. They are happy to let you tailor the trip but they'll make suggestions or plan it for you if you wish. You can decide whether you want to eat on board or at a beach bar or gourmet restaurant and whether you want to spend more time sailing or more time resting at anchor or snorkeling. The rate is $600 per day for one to four people. Half days (morning, afternoon, or into sunset) are $400 for one to four people. Overnight charters are $1,000 per night (two-night minimum) including your beverages.

Speedy's Ferry Service *(284.495.5240)* offers a day trip to Virgin Gorda from Road Town, which includes transportation to the Baths and lunch at the Bath & Turtle Restaurant. No advance reservation is needed. Just be at the dock before 9 am and be sure the boat you get on is Speedy's, not Smith's. The boat leaves at 9 am from the public ferry dock in Road Town and leaves Virgin Gorda for the trip back at 3:30 pm (4 pm on Sunday). Cost is $25 per person ($15 for children). This is a fairly inexpensive way to see Virgin Gorda and enjoy a nautical adventure.

Sunshine Pleasure Boats *(284.494.8813)* located at Village Cay Marina in Road Town offers a full menu of nautical choices. From bareboat rentals (center console 22' to 25'), to snorkeling trips, to captained fishing and island-hopping trips, they offer just about any nautical adventure you could imagine. Call for prices.

White Squall II (284.494.2564, www.whitesquall2.com) heads to the Baths on Virgin Gorda and Cooper Island or goes to Norman Island and the Indians. It's a traditional 80' schooner so there may be a lot of people but there is still plenty of room. Rates include a barbecue lunch with wine, rum punch, and beer, and complimentary snorkel equipment. The boat sails at 9:30 am from Village Cay Marina in Road Town. Rates are $100 per person.

GREAT FLY-FISHING
Many people don't know that there is excellent fly-fishing in the Caribbean. If this is one of your favorite sports, why not give it a try here?

Caribbean Fly-Fishing *(284.494.4797, www.caribflyfishing.com)* claims to have the best saltwater fly-fishing in the Caribbean. They will rendezvous with you whether you're at a hotel on land or on a charter boat. They'll take you in their Bertram 28' to proven fishing flats, transfer you to a custom flats skiff, and you and your guide will begin your fishing adventure. You can bring your own equipment or they'll provide whatever you need. The full-day rate is $850, half-day $480, based on two people.

Remember, the Caribbean sun is stronger than up north—wear a hat and lots of sun block on your nautical adventure! And don't forget your camera.

SPAS, SPORTS, AND FITNESS ON TORTOLA

GOLF

It's not exactly golf, but if you feel like practicing your drive into the ocean, stop by **Captain Mulligan's Golf Driving Range** *(284.494.0602)* at Nanny Cay.

HIKING

Trails to Sage Mountain National Park show off a great view from the highest point on Tortola, 1,780'. You can also hike from Brewer's Bay to Mount Healthy National Park where there is a restored 18th-century windmill. It's a great place for a picnic.

HORSEBACK RIDING

Shadow has very gentle horses and will take two to six people on guided rides to Brewer's Bay, Cane Garden Bay, and along Ridge Road. Instruction is also available. Call Shadow at **Shadow's Stables** *(284.494.2262)* on Ridge Road just east of Skyworld. Do wear long pants.

TENNIS

You'll find two courts at the **Long Bay Beach Resort** *(284.495.4252)* and non-hotel guests are welcome at both for a nominal charge.

SPAS, THERAPEUTIC MASSAGE, AND YOGA

When you want to cool down and be pampered, you'll find some soothing spas on Tortola. Be sure to call ahead for appointments.

The Spa at Long Bay *(284.495.4252 or 284.494.0138)* at Long Bay Beach Resort has a full menu of body wraps and offers therapeutic massage, facials, manicures, and saunas. In Road Town, the **Oasis** *(284.494.8891)* can take care of everything from hair color to foil highlights to acrylic nails and body wraps.

The inviting **Almond Tree Salon & Day Spa** *(284.495.4208)* at Nanny Cay (halfway between West End and Road Town) is the place to go for a great haircut (men or women) or hair color. It's the winner of the Best Hair Stylist and Best Hair Colorist in both the USVI and BVI.

At **Fort Recovery** *(284.495.4467)*, Pamelah Jacobson and her staff specialize in a combination of Swedish, Shiatsu, and Reflexology massage. Yoga classes are given by appointment (24-hour notice please).

A "SMUGGLER'S" ADVENTURE

Smuggler's Cove is an out-of-the-way, beautiful beach with good snorkeling and calm water for swimming. It's on the northwest shore of Tortola about eight bumpy minutes from the Long Bay Beach Resort.

This is one of Tortola's most beautiful and most protected beaches. There is a good snorkeling reef that you can easily spot from land. The best snorkeling is out from the shore a bit, just before the little waves are breaking. Those who have been here before will be sad to learn that "Uncle Bob," who ran the Caribbean's most unusual little snack bar, complete with a 1960 Lincoln Continental, passed away in 2002.

Steven's Beach Bar, a tiny stand tucked in the seagrapes, is open most days and serves hot dogs, chips, fruits, island drinks, and beer and sodas and even rents snorkel gear here. But don't forget to bring sunscreen and drinking water.

Directions: Get yourself to Long Bay Beach Resort. The road from here to Smuggler's is almost all dirt but passable (although not necessarily comfortable because of the bumps) in a car although a jeep-type vehicle with a lot of clearance is preferable, especially if it is muddy. The drive takes only about eight minutes but it will seem longer the first time.

Follow the road past Long Bay Beach Resort. Eventually the road veers abruptly left. Start driving up the hill but look for the very first right. It's hard to spot and the turn is abrupt and drops sharply down. However, it's just before the sign for Belmont Estates. (This is one of the most exclusive areas of Tortola and there are many luxurious homes and villas tucked up in these hills.) Take this right, which spills quickly down. Be patient and go slowly. The road ahead is dirt, deeply rutted, and has giant potholes and rocks that can blow a tire, so you have to kind of pick your way around obstacles.

This road winds through tangles of second-growth forest and is woodsy and shady. (You're driving inland a bit to get around a large salt pond.) When the road finally bears right, you'll be in the parking area for Smuggler's Cove. You may see a few other cars, but if you are lucky, you could be the only one.

Returning is a little difficult because there are several turns that lead to nowhere but that look seductively "right." Just keep bearing left whenever you have a choice and eventually you will be back on the road that leads past Long Bay. (When you come to the sign that points right to "Long Bay" you can go right or left. Both roads lead to the road back to Long Bay.)

TORTOLA'S TOWNS

If you look at Tortola's curvy shoreline from a plane, you'll see that it is defined by one bay after another. These bays have become Tortola's "landmarks" and the names of Tortola's settlements. People live in Sea Cows Bay, or Carrot Bay, or Baughers Bay, or Soper's Hole. The bays are used to indicate location and you will encounter bay names far more frequently than road names when you ask for directions.

The only big town is Road Town. West End (also referred to as Soper's Hole or Frenchman's Cay) is little and Trellis Bay at the east end is tiny.

GREAT SHOPPING IN ROAD TOWN

There are many wonderful places to shop in Road Town but they are scattered about (although within easy walking distance from each other). Bear in mind that this is the capital of a country and also by far the country's biggest town. Islanders come here from all over Tortola and from all of the other British Virgin Islands for almost everything they need—from hammers to Scotch tape to drivers' licenses. It can be extremely trafficky during weekdays.

Road Town has no separate "tourist" area with a nice little row of boutiques and eateries. It is a real place, with restaurants, bars, and shops tucked in between hardware stores and government agencies. The islanders dress up when they come to Road Town because it is their "city." It's okay for visitors to be casually dressed but bathing suits or short shorts in town are unacceptable. Also, don't be intimidated by a shabby storefront door. Paint and metal are simply no match for the Caribbean sun, wind, and salt air.

GREAT ROAD TOWN SHOPS

There are two main shopping areas in Road Town: Main Street and Wickham's Cay I. Locals use landmarks for directions so it really helps to know the major ones. In Road Town, when you ask where something is, it's usually near Scotia Bank or the roundabout or Bobby's (a supermarket) or Bolo's (next to Bobby's). See the map on page 80 for locations. Bolo's, by the way, is an excellent source for everything from batteries to cosmetics.

Great Main Street Shops

These stores are listed in geographical order, beginning at the Post Office.
Esme's Shop *(284.494.3961)*, across from the Post Office, is the place to come when you start feeling "out of touch" and want U.S. newspapers and magazines.

Kaunda's Kysy Tropix 2 *(284.494.6737)* carries DVDs and a huge selection of CDs: reggae, rap, rock, hip hop, punk, steel bands, and today's hits.

Samarkand *(284.494.6415)* handcrafts gold and silver jewelry. Many pieces have an island motif—sand dollars, shells, anchors—and make perfect gifts.

The Gallery *(284.494.6680)* displays stunning island photographs by Amanda Baker and lovely paintings of island scenes by Lisa Gray. Bring one home and be reminded of the BVI every single day! Check out the coasters and note cards.

Pusser's Company Store *(284.494.2467)* is home to two floors of attractive and comfortable clothing for the whole family, bottles of their famous rum, nautical antiques, island books, postcards, and much, much more!

Jewellery Box *(284.494.7278)* showcases gold and silver jewelry and one-of-a-kind pieces fashioned out of shells, wood, and the local sandbox plant.

Latitude 18 *(284.494.7807)*, located at Main Street's major curve, carries colorful sportswear and island wear for the whole family. There are great T-shirts, sunglasses, sundresses, pants, shorts, backpacks, bathing suits, sarongs, and rows and rows of great hats. A branch is located at Frenchman's Cay.

Hucksters *(284.494.7165)*, in the old Customs House, offers a delightful selection of hand-painted pottery, glassware and china decorated with island motifs, colorful placemats, attractive greeting cards, Caribbean books, and beautiful antique maps. Wares are artfully displayed on tables and shelves and the more you look the more you will find. A sister shop is at Frenchman's Cay.

Sunny Caribbee Herb and Spice Co. *(284.494.2178)* is the place for wonderful exotic spices, "hangover cures," island books, cookbooks, handmade jewelry, island art, and colorful pottery, including some delightful items from the BVI's Bamboushay and Barbados Earthworks. Anything you buy can be shipped home for you.

Serendipity *(284.494.5865)* features an eclectic mix of coffee table books, best-sellers, popular fiction, island books, and interesting nonfiction plus note cards and an appealing selection of miniature books.

Great Shopping on Wickhams Cay I

Books Etcetera *(284.494.6611)*, tucked in the marina side of the Mill Mall complex, features *The New York Times* hardcover best-sellers, current newspapers including *The New York Times* and *Wall Street Journal*, U.S. magazines, paperbacks, postcards, and beautiful maps of the islands.

Cantik *(284.494.7927)* is a bit hidden (walk out on the dock towards the Captain's Table) but a delight. Come to this outstanding shop for beautiful handmade greeting cards, island music CDs, wind chimes, candles, clocks embedded in polished wood, watches, fabric, exotic incenses, unusual pottery, and furniture. (Walk through to the back room to see everything.) Look for the perfectly tuned tiny steel drum. Anything you buy can be shipped anywhere.

Crafts Alive, a collection of pastel-painted West Indian cottages in a park-like setting overlooking Road Town Harbour, is a good place to come for T-shirts, hats, jewelry, and locally made hot sauces and craft items. Each cottage has something different to offer. This area can be crowded when cruise ships are in and many cottages close on non-cruise ship days.

D'Zandra's Black Coral Jewelry *(284.494.4717)*, on the marina side of the Mill Mall complex, is a showcase for earrings, bracelets, pendants, and other jewelry items crafted out of black coral scraps washed up by the sea. Look for the outstanding coral sculptures of a crab and of a lobster.

Ample Hamper *(284.494.2494)* is a complete grocery store with a deli and a sundries section (suntan lotion, bug repellent) and has a very large selection of wines. A smaller branch is at Frenchman's Cay. **Bobby's** *(284.495.2140)* is a full-service grocery store offering just about everything. See map for location.

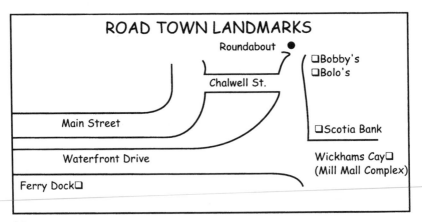

ROAD TOWN LANDMARKS

80

GREAT SHOPPING IN FRENCHMAN'S CAY AT WEST END

West End actually refers to the area along the north shore of Soper's Hole, a deep anchorage at the West End of Tortola, where you will find the Customs Office, public ferry docks, Zelma's Variety, and the Jolly Roger Bar and Restaurant. Across the water, on an island called Frenchman's Cay that is connected to the mainland by a bridge, is a small collection of appealing shops and a restaurant.

When you feel like food or a drink, stop at **Pusser's** *for a salad or sandwich or their famous painkiller punch or drop into* **Pices** *for burgers and conch fritters.*

Blue Water Divers *(284.495.1200)* carries bathing suits that let the sun through so you can tan all over, plus diving and snorkeling gear and island books.

Culture Classic Boutique *(284.494.6415)* is a tiny shop full of gauzy dresses, colorful sarongs, unusual wind chimes, postcards, and T-shirts.

Caribbean Jewellers *(284.495.4137)*, a branch of Road Town's Samarkand, displays delicate 14K gold and silver jewelry.

Harbour Market *(284.495.4541)* is a delightful grocery with just about everything you might need, from gourmet cheeses, to garlic and spices, to fresh vegetables, to racks and racks of excellent wines. There's a deli, too.

Hucksters *(284.495.3087)*, with a sister shop in Road Town, showcases decorative housewares such as pretty placemats and napkins and hand-painted glassware, plus island books, knicknacks, and unusual finds.

Latitude 18 *(284.494.7807)* features colorful Caribbean clothing for the whole family. Come here for bathing suits, backpacks, hats, sarongs, sundresses, T-shirts, sunglasses, and more. A sister shop is on Main Street in Road Town.

Pusser's Company Store *(284.495.4554)* carries clothing for everyone in the family plus their famous rum, nautical items, and island books.

Zenida *(284.495.4867)* is the place to come for exotic items from around the world. Look for colorful fabrics, bedspreads, sarongs, wood carvings, unusual jewelry, carry-alls, and much more in this tiny store.

GREAT SHOPPING ELSEWHERE

Aragorn's Studio *(284.495.1849)*, facing Trellis Bay just past the airport, displays Caribbean arts and crafts, including island music, unusual pieces of jewelry, artist-designed T-shirts, books, and clothing for women. Check out the dramatic sculptures of birds and sea creatures. Custom-made copper sculptures can be ordered. If you are on island for a while, take a look at the schedule for pottery, wood carving, basketry, and painting lessons.

Bamboushay *(284.494.0393)*, at Nanny Cay (halfway between Road Town and West End), is the location for beautifully created local pottery. Here are stunning bowls, vases, plates, and platters plus paintings by local artists. Anything you buy can be shipped home or you can have something custom-made and shipped to you on completion.

Elegant Pelican *(284.495.4252)*, next to reception at Long Bay Beach Resort, is worth a visit no matter where you are staying. This charming two-story boutique carries an outstanding collection of resortwear for men and women. You'll find great shirts and shorts, wrap skirts, and bathing suits and cover-ups plus unusual Caribbean art, island books and paperbacks, and handsome T-shirts and hats. Go up the stairs! It's worth it!

Fluke's Gallery *(284.495.2043)*, on Trellis Bay just past the airport, is the place to purchase these delightful and well-known island prints by Roger F. Ellis. Look also for the very delicate botanical prints.

Jan's Potporri *(284.495.4837)*, at Quito's in Cane Garden Bay, carries delightful, one-of-a-kind cover-ups, satchels, and beach bags, plus candles and bathing suits.

Olivia's Store *(284.495.9649)*, on Cane Garden Bay next to Myett's, sells postcards, maps, many gift items, island artwork, books, T-shirts, sarongs, cover-ups, plus film and suntan lotion.

Skyworld Boutique *(284.494.3567)*, at Skyworld restaurant *(see page 85)*, is tiny but has a bit of everything, from local artwork to Sunny Caribbee spices, including special coffees and teas.

Sporting Pelican *(284.495.4252)*, on the beach at Long Bay Beach Resort, carries a large collection of shorts and T-shirts, including many by Hi Ho plus swim gear, boogie boards, suntan lotion, and sunglasses.

TORTOLA'S GREAT RESTAURANTS AND BARS

One of the extraordinary things about dining in the islands is that most of the time you are outside. Many restaurants simply don't have walls. A canopy or roof protects you from the occasional cloudburst. In addition, many dining areas overlook the water. It is possible to get anything from a hamburger to an elegant, four-course meal in this kind of exotic setting. Restaurants below are organized geographically (see map page 88) *and are open daily unless stated otherwise.*

IN AND NEAR ROAD TOWN

Brandywine Bay Restaurant *(284.495.2301)*, an easy 10-minute cab ride from Road Town, is set on a hilltop overlooking the water and is one of the BVI's finest restaurants. Dine by candlelight inside or outside on one of several romantic terraces. Italian owner/chef Davide Pugliese flies in ingredients from all over the world, buys the best local fish, and makes his own mozzarella. Australian owner Cele manages the restaurant and gracefully presents the nightly version of the ever-changing menu, which offers a number of appetizers, entrees, and dessert choices. This is the place to come if you like fresh mussels, beef carpaccio, Peking roast duck with raspberry sauce, filet mignon with porcini mushroom sauce, stuffed veal chops, grilled tuna, lemon tarts, and chocolate walnut torte served in a sophisticated setting. The wine list has superb Italian and Australian selections. *Reservations a must. Casual elegant (long pants, collared shirt for men). Closed early-Aug. to late-Oct. and Sun. D $$$*

C&F *(284.494.4941)*, at Purcell Estate just outside Road Town, is run by Clarence, a well-known local chef, and his wife, Florence. It's packed nightly. People come for generous platters of fresh local swordfish and lobster, tasty barbecued ribs, fried plantains, conch fritters, and curry. This is a brightly lit, ultracasual place, full of diners obviously enjoying their meals. *D $$-$$$*

Capriccio di Mare *(284.494.5369)*, on Waterfront Drive, is an authentic outdoor Italian cafe and the cuisine here is superb. In the morning sip espresso and munch on Italian pastries. Come back around noon and choose from a huge selection of salads, crostinis, focaccia, pastas, and pizzas. Try the insalata mista, spaghetti arrabbiati, or spaghetti puttanesca, or penne caprese. Return in the evening for a pizza margherita! The house specialty is a delicious Mango Bellini, a variation of the Bellini cocktail served at Harry's Bar in Venice and there are some good Italian red and white wines. Owners are Davide and Cele Pugliese of Brandywine Bay fame. *Closed Sun. BLD $$*

Captain's Table *(284.494.3885)*, in Road Town on Wickham's Cay I, offers fine dining inside or outside on the slim veranda facing the harbor. The tablecloths are red-and-white checked and the lighting is dim at this popular spot. The French chef has created an outstanding French and Continental menu. In addition, two blackboards offer a huge number of tempting lunch specials and an equally large number of appealing dinner specials. Choices run the gamut from homemade soups, fresh salads, and a multitude of sandwiches and light meals at lunch to vegetarian dishes, veal and chicken creations, grilled steaks, pasta dishes, and more in the evening. You can also choose your own fresh live lobster right out of their lobster pool. (Just watch out you don't fall in—the pool is right in the floor in the middle of the dining room.) *L (Mon.-Fri.), D $$$*

Le Cabanon *(284.494.8660)*, on Waterfront Drive, serves authentic French fare in a very casual open-air setting. Good lunch choices include the quiche Lorraine, the ham and cheese omelette, the goat cheese salad, the croque monsieur, or the chorizo and brie sandwich. Come back for great dinner selections, such as a grilled filet, duck prepared various ways, and fresh fish. You can't go wrong at this popular French bistro. *Closed Sun. L (Mon.-Fri.), D $$*

The Dove *(284.494.0313)*, on Waterfront Drive, is in a charming West Indian cottage and one of Tortola's finest restaurants. The deep red walls contrast nicely with the white tablecloths and the setting is truly elegant. The menu changes seasonally but might include starters such as foie gras pizza, eggplant potstickers, and softshell crab tempura. Entrees could be grilled wild boar sausage, basil pesto ravioli, or coffee and pecan-seared beef tenderloin. Sushi and an excellent cheese board are offered, too. Come early and sip champagne at the handsome bar or amidst the tropical foliage on the outdoor deck. *Reservations a must. Closed Mon. D $$$*

The Pub *(284.494.2608)*, across from Fort Burt, has a pleasant terrace facing Road Harbour and the views are great day and night. Head to this popular, very casual place for barbecued ribs and chicken, curried conch, fish and chips, and burgers. For breakfast try the great pancakes. *Opens 5 pm Sun. BLD $$*

Pusser's Pub *(284.494.3897)* is almost always hopping. Stop here for Pusser's famous painkillers plus fish & chips, deli sandwiches, burgers and pizzas. Young crowds head here Thursdays for "nickel beer night." *LD $-$$*

Roti Palace *(284.494.4196)*, on Main Street (above Samarkand), serves some of the best rotis on Tortola. (Properly made rotis are curries wrapped in a delicate, garlicky flat bread.) Dine inside or on the breezy veranda and choose from lobster, whelk, conch, beef, or chicken (boneless is better). *LD $-$$*

Skyworld *(284.494.3567)*, about 10 minutes straight up from Road Town on Ridge Road, offers fine dining with a spectacular view (if you get here before dark). Windows in the all-white hexagonal dining room showcase hills and distant islands and the cuisine is excellent. Start with goat cheese over baby greens or conch fritters. Move on to yellowfin tuna with mango-avocado salsa or roast pork tenderloin with Pernod honey-ginger jus or macadamia nut-crusted chicken breast. Save room for the whiskey walnut tart. The simple lunch menu features curry wraps, burgers, sandwiches and salads. *Reservations. LD $$-$$$*

Spaghetti Junction *(284.494.4880)*, four minutes east of Road Town, has long been one of Tortola's most popular spots. Broad steps lead up to a rather grand dining space, with peach walls, dark wood furniture, columns and chandeliers, and numerous windows open to the breezes. Candlelit tables sit between tropical plants. The service and cuisine are delightful, thanks to owners John Schultheiss and April Ridi. Try the delicious bruschetta or tasty mozzarella sticks first. Entree choices include an outstanding osso bucco, spaghetti and meatballs, jambalaya pasta, and beef filet with a marsala wine sauce. Save room for the chocolate mousse and some energy for late-night partying that goes on at the Bat Cave (just beyond the bar). *Reservations. Closed Sept. and closed Sun. D $$.*

Virgin Queen *(284.494.2310)*, upstairs near the roundabout, is where locals and the yachting crowd gather for stouts, ales, and lagers as well as bangers and mash, shepherd's pie, fish and chips, local dishes like salt fish, mutton stew, and peas and rice and the famous Queen's Pizza. *LD $-$$*

WEST END
Coco Plums *(284.495.4672)*, in Apple Bay, is a tiny little restaurant open to some breezes. It's run by a pair of energetic chefs who have fun with the menu. Try their vodoo ribs or the rasta pasta. Other pastas include chicken pesto and shrimp Alfredo. There's also a stuffed chicken breast and a grilled N.Y. steak. Lunches include conch fritters and burgers. *No lunch Sat. BLD $$*

The "Fish Fry" is on Zion Hill Road in Apple Bay. This is an outdoor gathering (there's no sign). Every Friday and Saturday evening locals stoke up the fires by the side of the road and cook excellent local fish here. It's a minute or so walk from Sebastian's and Little Apple Bay on Tortola's North Shore. *D $*

Jolly Roger *(284.495.4559)*, at West End past the ferry dock, is an extremely casual delight. Sit on the little upstairs terrace and have a breakfast of French toast or eggs your way. The conch fritters, rotis, and pizzas are great. So is the tuna with ginger soy sauce and the beef tenderloin with a brandy-mushroom demi-glace. Saturday there's a barbecue. *Closed Aug.-Sept. BLD $-$$*

Mrs. Scatliffe's *(284.495.4556)* is on Carrot Bay. Known as the queen of local cooking, she serves family-style meals in her home every evening. Menus change nightly, but might include curried goat, pot roast pork, chicken and coconut, and conch fritters. *Reservations necessary by 5:30 pm. D $$*

The Palm Terrace *(284.495.4252)*, at Long Bay Beach Resort, offers an elegant setting. Tables are on several levels, all lit by candles and open to the breezes. The menu changes nightly but might include a choice of roasted red pepper soup, salad, or sauteed sea scallops first, then a choice of filet with a port wine sauce, roasted cornish game hen with ratatouille, grilled swordfish, and a vegetarian special. Desserts are a delight, especially the chocolate mousse. You might want to arrive early to enjoy a beverage on the adjoining, very pleasant garden terrace. *Reservations a must. Casual elegant. Closed Sun. on season. Check for off-season schedule. D $$$*

Pices *(284.495.3154)*, on Frenchman's Cay, has a casual outdoor terrace as well as a simple indoor dining room. Have a lunch of conch fritters, burgers, Caesar salad, or honey-stung chicken. At dinner, try the curried shrimp, jerk chicken breast, or fresh catch. Breakfast is good, too, from the omelette to eggs Benedict to French toast. *BLD $-$$*

Pusser's Landing *(284.495.4554)*, on Frenchman's Cay, is a popular lunch stop for burgers and pizzas and, of course, Pusser's famous painkillers. *LD $-$$*

Sebastian's On the Beach *(284.495.4212)*, at Apple Bay, is a casual, excellent place for breakfast (fresh fruit, eggs, pancakes) or lunch (burgers, sandwiches, conch fritters, outstanding vegetarian rotis, and salads). The best tables are on the breezy terrace overhanging the beach with superb views of pelicans diving for fish and, at night, the twinkling lights of Jost Van Dyke. Dinner (grilled lobster, local fish, steaks) is very informal but can be quite romantic. *Call ahead for lobster. BLD $-$$*

Sugar Mill *(284.495.4355)*, in Apple Bay, is a romantic spot. The setting is lovely, in a restored 360-year-old sugar mill with beautiful stonework walls and tables lit by candles. The menu changes nightly, with a choice of several appetizers, salads, entrees, and desserts. Black bean and roasted pumpkin soup, Hoisin duck in a scallion pancake, and chipotle chicken sausage are typical appetizers, and for the main course, grilled local fish with mango salsa, filet mignon with sun-dried tomato Bernaise sauce, mustard-crusted rack of lamb, and a vegetarian dish such as pumpkin and black bean lasagna. Come early for a drink in the lovely outdoor gazebo. *Reservations a must. Smart casual (dress shorts okay for men). Closed Aug.-Sept. D $$-$$$*

CANE GARDEN BAY
Big Banana Club Paradise *(284.495.4606)*, on the beach at Cane Garden Bay, offers sandwiches, pizza, ice cream, and great island drinks. *LD $-$$*

Myett's Garden and Grill *(284.495.9649)*, at Cane Garden Bay, is a casual, barefoot sort of place that can be somewhat frenetic. Burgers, salads, and wraps are served at lunch. Dinner features ribs, chicken, and lobster. *LD $-$$*

Quito's Gazebo *(284.495.4837)*, at the east end of Cane Garden Bay, is owned by recording star Quito Rhymer and is a great place to enjoy burgers and rotis at lunch and ribs, conch, and local fish West Indian style for dinner. Barbecues are Sundays and Wednesdays. Tuesday and Thursday evenings, Quito performs solo and Friday and Saturday he entertains with his band. *LD $-$$*

EAST END AND TRELLIS BAY
D' Best Cup *(284.495.0259)*, at Trellis Bay, may be tiny but the food is terrific. Try the the escargot or the little crab cakes or seared tuna or roast beef on a baguette with melted cheese and onions. There are specialty teas and coffees, and excellent breakfast choices, too. *BL $*

Eclipse *(284.495.1646)*, at Penn's Landing, in an elegant setting over the water, features an eclectic menu: spring rolls, quesadillas, chicken skewers jerk Jamaican or Thai-seared, lobster ravioli, polenta with shiitake mushrooms and sun-dried tomatoes, or sesame tuna carpaccio. Many items are also available in small portions, so you can "graze" through dinner, ordering one at a time (some smalls are on the large size, so let the knowledgeable waitstaff be your guide). Flight aficionados will enjoy watching the little planes in final approach. *Closed Mon.; Sun. open for brunch only. D, Sun. Brunch $$-$$$*

Fat Hog Bob's *(284.495.1010)* is in Maya Cove. Beer banners hang from the ceiling at this appealing and spacious bar and restaurant, with handsome wood walls, a terrace overlooking the water, and the wine list on the table lampshades. Come here when you need an "Outback" fix: bloomin' onions and piles of French fries plus giant burgers, steaks, ribs, and local fish. *LD $$-$$$*

Tamarind Club *(284.495.2477)* sits high above Josiah's Bay and is very popular and worth a visit despite its somewhat remote location. Tables are spread about on a large open-air terrace. The extensive menu changes but starters might include panko-crusted brie, shrimp and corn fritters, or char-grilled romaine with warm bacon-balsamic dressing. The main courses could be jerk-rubbed pork tenderloin, tuna with wasabi sauce, or a seafood mixed grill. *Reservations a must, for dinner and for brunch. Closed Aug.-Sept. BLD, Sun. Brunch $$-$$$*

BEYOND TORTOLA'S EAST END

Pusser's Marina Cay *(284.494.2174)* has free ferry service *(schedules page 140)* from their dock on Beef Island to their restaurant on Marina Cay. The dinner menu features barbecued ribs, grilled steak, lobster, and fresh fish served in their al fresco beachside restaurant. *LD $$*

The Last Resort *(284.495.2520)* is actually on a tiny little islet just off Beef Island. Not only is there an eclectic menu of tapas, local seafood, and roast beef, there's also Tony Snell's popular after-dinner show. *D $$*

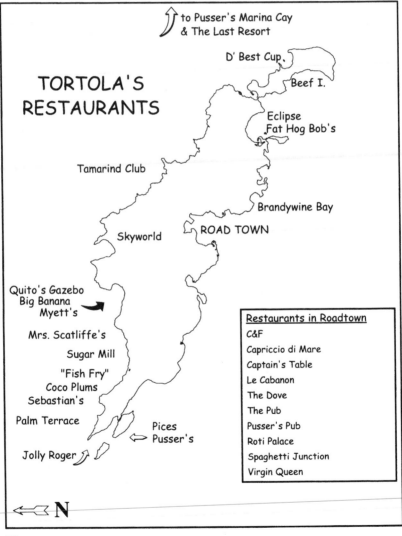

to Pusser's Marina Cay
& The Last Resort

D' Best Cup

TORTOLA'S
RESTAURANTS

Beef I.

Eclipse
Fat Hog Bob's

Tamarind Club

Brandywine Bay

Skyworld   ROAD TOWN

Quito's Gazebo
Big Banana
Myett's

Mrs. Scatliffe's

Sugar Mill

"Fish Fry"
Coco Plums
Sebastian's

Palm Terrace

Pices
Pusser's

Jolly Roger

Restaurants in Roadtown

C&F
Capriccio di Mare
Captain's Table
Le Cabanon
The Dove
The Pub
Pusser's Pub
Roti Palace
Spaghetti Junction
Virgin Queen

N

SOME TIPS ON BVI RESTAURANTS

❑Don't be alarmed if there aren't many other patrons in a restaurant. In the U.S. this generally means that you are in a bad place, but in the islands it is perfectly normal. In the islands there are just far fewer people around.

❑Contrary to popular thought, vegetables and fruits are not plentiful on these islands. (The rains are too uneven and the land too rocky.) Virtually all produce is shipped from the southern Caribbean, Puerto Rico, or from the States. If there is very little lettuce in your salad, it is probably because the restaurant is desperately waiting for a fresh shipment to come in on the next boat.

❑Fresh milk is shipped from St. Thomas and Puerto Rico and quickly turns in the Caribbean heat. Although you will see fresh milk in the supermarkets, virtually everyone relies on "Long Life" milk which comes in nonrefrigerated cartons and is usually from England.

❑Many visitors from the U.S. get frustrated by the peaceful pace of restaurant service, forgetting, of course, that the reason they came to the BVI in the first place was to slow down and relax. Enjoy the scenery and the pace. If you have to catch a plane or a boat, let someone know and they'll happily serve you more quickly.

❑Water is scarce on these islands. Islanders can last a week with the water people from the U.S. can waste in a day. Drinking water is rarely served unless requested.

❑Many restaurants serve American-style food, but it won't necessarily be exactly what you are expecting. Cooking styles are different here and supplies are limited.

GREAT NIGHTLIFE ON TORTOLA

On Friday and Saturday nights and Sunday afternoons many Tortola bars and restaurants feature live entertainment. However, you can usually find live music any night of the week, especially on season. BVI musicians often play at a different hotel or bar each night, so if you find a group you particularly like, find out where they will be playing next.

Many musicians travel back and forth between the islands but no one beats the travel feats of guitarist Ruben Chinnery, who often entertains on several islands in the course of a single afternoon and evening.

One of the great things about all of this music is that generally you are listening to it outside, under the blanket of Caribbean stars! Remember, bands do move around, so it's best to call the establishment to see which band will be there or to check the Limin' Times, *which comes out weekly, for up-to-the-minute schedules of who is playing where.*

Love Songs

For romantic sounds, be sure to find wonderful Ruben Chinnery, who hails from Jost Van Dyke and who plays the guitar and sings ballads and love songs. Or check out Quito, who plays love songs at his own restaurant in Cane Garden Bay, Quito's Gazebo.

Steel Bands

Do catch a steel band at least once—the music is quite beautiful and it's hard to believe these smooth mellow sounds are made by striking oil drums. This form of music originated in Trinidad but is now found all over the Caribbean. Great BVI steel bands include Pan-Vibes, the Shooting Stars, Romeo and the Injectors, and Lashing Dogs.

Fungi Bands

Fungi bands are a type of scratch band that combines flutes with washboards, bottles, gourds, and other household items. It's hard not to get caught up in the fun and rhythm of a fungi band! See if you can find the fungi bands Spark Plugs or The Lover Boys.

Reggae

O-2B and Xtreme play a kind of modernized Reggae plus contemporary top-40s and rock and roll—all great for shaking it up or dancing cheek-to-cheek.

TORTOLA NIGHTLIFE

Bat Cave *(inside Spaghetti Junction four minutes east of Road Town, 284.494.4880)*. It's jam-packed until way late at night at Tortola's hottest night spot. There's usually live entertainment Wednesdays and weekends.

Bomba's Shack *(Apple Bay, North Shore, 284.495.4148)*. Local bands play here Wednesday evenings and Sunday afternoons and at his famous all-night Full Moon and Blue Moon parties.

Fat Hog Bob's *(Maya Cove, East End, 284.495.1010)* features bands Friday nights.

Jolly Roger *(Soper's Hole, West End, 284.495.4559)*. Come for live bands and a barbecue every Friday and Saturday (and sometimes Thursday).

Long Bay Beach Resort *(Long Bay, North Shore, 284.495.4252)*. Generally, the Tuesday night barbecue features the steel band Pan-Vibes and the Third Dimension plays at the Friday barbecue but barbecue nights and bands can vary.

Myett's *(Cane Garden Bay, North Shore 284.495.9649)*. Friday, Saturday, Sunday, and Monday nights local bands keep this popular spot hopping.

Quito's Gazebo *(Cane Garden Bay, North Shore, 284.495.4837)*. Recording star Quito Rymer plays guitar and sings his love songs and ballads every Tuesday and Thursday and entertains with his band Quito and the Edge Friday and Saturday.

Sebastian's *(Apple Bay, North Shore, 284.495.4212)*. Frequently a local band plays here on weekends. Often, Saturday night it's the steel band Pan-Vibes, and Sunday it's the fungi band The Spark Plugs.

BOMBA'S SHACK

Most everybody has heard of Bomba by now. His Full Moon parties are famous throughout the Caribbean. Drive by the place during the day and you might mistake it for a junk pile, but Wednesdays, Sundays, and full moon nights the place, and the beach and fields around it, are packed. You can stop here any day any time after 10 am and try Bomba's specialty, a blend of passionfruit, guava, banana, papaya, pineapple, and orange juices mixed with Bomba's homemade rum—a secret recipe handed down by his family.

WONDERFUL SIGHTS AT NIGHT

Shooting stars. Just stare at the night sky for a few minutes and you're bound to catch a shooting star. Some shooting stars streak high across the sky but others are so big and fall so close they'll take your breath away.

Satellites. Stare up at the sky and watch for a satellite. This can take some patience, but eventually you will see one making its way across the nighttime canopy. It will look like an airplane way up high, but without the telltale red and green blinking lights of a plane.

Southern Cross. Many think this is visible only from the southern hemisphere but in June and July, especially if you are on a hilltop in the BVI looking south, you can catch this legendary constellation just above the horizon. There's no mistaking this one when you see it.

Glitter in the water. Catch the sparkling phosphorescence. Streak a stick through the water at the edge of a dark dock, or watch your paddle stir up glitter on a nighttime kayak ride, or watch water gently lapping against the shore, especially on a moonless night when there is less competing light.

Underwater sights. Go on a night dive or a night snorkel. It's completely different from a daytime underwater adventure and truly unbelievable to see how many "electric" creatures dance around in the nighttime ocean.

A LIST OF WHAT NOT TO MISS

❑Dinner at Brandywine Bay or The Dove

❑Stopping by Bamboushay to see the beautiful pottery that is handcrafted on site

❑A visit to at least one Pusser's store

❑Joining in the late-night revelry at the ever-popular Bat Cave

❑At least one snorkel, anywhere

❑Browsing through the Elegant Pelican at Long Bay Beach Resort for great swimwear, classy men's and women's casual clothing, sandals, local pottery, and souvenirs

❑The view from Skyworld

❑A cappuccino or a Mango Bellini or a bowl of penne with spicy tomato sauce at Capriccio di Mare in Road Town

❑Taking at least one nautical adventure, from renting a dinghy to going on a day sail

❑Breakfast at Sebastian's, watching the pelicans dive-bomb for their morning repast

❑Being serenaded by Quito, live and in person, Tuesday or Thursday evening on Cane Garden Bay

TORTOLA'S GREAT LODGING CHOICES

On Tortola, you can stay in everything from a full-service resort to smaller inn-like lodging to villas and you might want to think about location. Several places to stay are scattered on the western end of the island. These West End lodgings each have their own restaurants, and, despite some extremely steep hills, are within a few minutes by car or taxi from various restaurants and bars and some shopping. Cane Garden Bay is unique in that it is one strip of beach lined with a number of little beach bars. It's an extremely popular anchorage and lively day and night. Brewer's Bay and Josiah's Bay are quite remote, Beef Island slightly less so.

Rates are per night for two people without meals on season, and do not include service charge (usually 10%) and 7% government tax. Prices ranges reflect different levels of accommodations. Off-season rates are in parentheses.

West End Lodging
FORT RECOVERY ESTATE

Pamelah Jacobson makes this cozy spot what it is—a great place to chill out, cool down, and simply recover from the stresses of stateside life.

Right on a smallish beach five minutes from West End by car is this very casual mini-resort that looks south toward Frenchman's Cay and St. John in the USVI. You drive through a gate and slip into a private and relaxing world full of brilliant tropical flowers. There is one beachfront three-bedroom villa, a two-bedroom villa, a one-bedroom poolside villa, and two floors of comfortable one- and two-bedroom apartments facing the water. These are staggered and balconies are fairly private. Interiors are bright and easy to live in, with small but full kitchens, air-conditioned bedrooms, separate living areas, and TVs. Penthouse apartments are on the second floor and have beamed cathedral ceilings and an airy feel. VCRs and videos can be rented. A restaurant just for resident guests offers breakfast, lunch, and dinner. Dinner can be served to you in your living room or on your terrace, course by course. The beach is smallish but very calm and good for swimming and snorkeling and there is a dock and an appealing swimming pool. Water sports, yoga, and massage therapy are available on site and boat trips can be arranged.

30 units. Rates for one-bedroom units (with continental breakfast): $250-$360 ($187-$236). Manager: Pamelah Jills Jacobson. Res: 800.367.8455. Tel: 284.495.4467. Fax: 284.495.4036. www.fortrecovery.com.

94

LONG BAY BEACH RESORT & VILLAS

A spectacular mile-long beach, pool, tennis courts, two appealing restaurants, and a full-service spa make this 52-acre resort (which is the closest to a full-service resort on Tortola) a place you never need to leave, but it's also a great location if you want to explore—it's easy to go to Smuggler's Cove or West End or even to hop over to Jost Van Dyke.

Tucked behind the sea grape trees along the beach are cozy rooms on stilts and also spacious deluxe units with large balconies and walk-in showers. Sea grapes are between these deluxe units and the beach and the second-floor units have better views. Scattered up the hillside are studios with Jacuzzis, poolside studios (top floor units have cathedral ceilings and feel more spacious), and one-, two-, and three-bedroom villas with full kitchens. The hillside is steep and views from many poolside and hillside units are stunning (and the walk from the beach or dinner is superb exercise). Units have air-conditioned bedrooms, phones, coffee makers, refrigerators, and TVs. For dinner the Palm Terrace Restaurant *(see page 86)* is a good choice and the casual 1748 Restaurant serves breakfast and lunch and has excellent barbecues. There is a pool and snack bar, two tennis courts, two neat shops (Elegant Pelican, Sporting Pelican), and a spa. *115 units. Rates: $250-$645 ($175-$350), villas more. Res.: 800.943.4699. Tel: 284.495.4252. Fax: 914.833.3318. www.longbay.com.*

SEBASTIAN'S SEASIDE VILLAS

Look out at great views of azure water and Caribbean islands and pelicans diving for dinner from these upscale and comfortable efficiencies built right above the water's edge and near an excellent casual restaurant.

These nine efficiencies are in a two-story building that overlooks the water just past the edge of narrow Apple Bay beach. All units are nicely decorated with dark wood furniture, pale yellow walls, and framed prints and have contemporary marble bathrooms and a cozy kitchenette with toaster, microwave, sink, and little fridge. Sliding glass doors stretch the length of the room, showcase stunning views, and open onto a private narrow balcony. The second-story rooms have cathedral ceilings and feel especially spacious. All units have ceiling fans, air-conditioning, and cable TV. Sebastian's restaurant *(see page 86)* is a delightful stop for breakfast, lunch, and dinner and there is also a bar and live entertainment some nights. Sebastian's also has 12 small beachfront rooms that are very basically furnished but can be a good value. Call for rates. By the way, Sebastian's is a short walk from Bomba's Shack, and you should stay here during a full moon only if you want to be part of Bomba's Full Moon Party. *9 units. Rates: $275-$325 ($150-$250), two-bedroom suite $550 ($350-$500). Tel: 284.495.4003. Fax: 284.495.4466. www.sebastiansvillas.com*

THE SUGAR MILL

Stay here when you want a simple yet sophisticated hideaway with a little patch of beach and a truly excellent restaurant. You can spend your days reading and resting or use it as a cozy base from which to explore.

Comfortable, air-conditioned rooms spill down the hillside at this intimate north shore spot on Apple Bay. Each has a little kitchen with a fridge and microwave and a private balcony with ocean views through the trees. There are two spacious two-bedroom Plantation House Suites (the upstairs one has a cathedral ceiling) and a two-bedroom villa with a full kitchen. These three have TV/VCRs. A 360-year-old sugar mill with handsome stone walls provides the appealing setting for reception, casual breakfasts, a little bar, and fine dining in the well-known Sugar Mill *(see page 86)*. Islands, a little beach grill, serves burgers, salads, and West Indian dishes for lunch, and Tuesday through Saturday on season, West Indian-inspired dinner items. The petite beach across the street offers calm swimming and good snorkeling. It's tiny but private, as nonguests rarely stop here. You can also take a dip in the circular pool.
Closed Aug., Sept. 24 units, including suites and villa. Rates: rooms $325-$355 ($240-$280), suites $650 ($565), villa $665 ($520). Res: 800.462.8834. Tel: 284.495-4355. Fax: 284.495.4696. www.sugarmillhotel.com

Cane Garden Bay Lodging
THE HERITAGE INN

Perched on Windy Hill high above Carrot Bay, these very basic suites offer extraordinary views, value, and the Bananakeet Cafe.

One- and two-bedroom units are in a motel-like structure high on a hill. They are modestly furnished, have king beds, air-conditioning, and kitchenettes with microwave, blender, and coffee maker. This simple inn has its own pool, a little boutique, and a small open-air restaurant. It's a comfortable, friendly "headquarters" from which to explore the island.
9 units. Rates: $175-$275 ($120-$175). Tel: 284.494.5842. Fax: 284.495.4100. www.heritageinnbvi.com.

THE OLE WORKS INN
The location on Cane Garden Bay is the draw here.
Rooms are very modest but Tortola's most famous beach is across the street. The main building is a 300-year-old restored sugar mill. Some units look out to the beach; others into the hills. There is also a honeymoon tower and a small pool.
18 units. Rates: $145-$185 ($80-$135). Tel: 284.495.4837. Fax 284.495.9618. www.quitorymer.com

LIGHTHOUSE VILLAS

Just a few steep steps above Cane Garden Bay's beach, Malcia Rymer Bean has created a delightful Caribbean escape with beautifully decorated, comfortable living areas and captivating views.

Suites here are spacious, clean and crisp, and very liveable. All are tastefully decorated in soft colors, have balconies overlooking the bay, fully equipped kitchens, air conditioning, and ceiling fans. This is a great choice if you want real comfort just a few steps from the watersports, dining, and entertainment found on Tortola's most famous beach.

6 suites. Weekly rates: $1225-$1995 ($735-$1400). Tel: 284.494.5482. Fax: 284.495.9101. www.travel-watch.com/lighthouse

Brewer's Bay Lodging
ICIS VILLAS

Located in a beautiful green valley a short walk from Brewer's Bay, this remote and comfortable hideaway with its own restaurant is a good choice for couples or families or anyone seeking isolation and a great beach.

Brewer's Bay is one of the more difficult places to get to on Tortola (lots of steep hills and unmarked roads) and it is a surprise to find this delightful oasis tucked in the greenery a short walk from the western edge of Brewer's Bay beach. The grounds are stunning, with lush tropical foliage, 60-year-old mahogany trees, and 100-year-old mango trees. The restaurant and reception are built around the remains of the first Baptist church in the BVI and the ancient stone walls are remarkable. A two-story motel-like structure houses comfortable, one-, two-, and three-bedroom suites. All have air-conditioned bedrooms, separate living/dining areas with full kitchens, cable TV, and a terrace. There are also two efficiencies, each with a kitchen. Spend the day relaxing by the waterfall and lovely landscaped pool or take the three-minute walk to the beach. The hotel restaurant serves breakfast and dinner. A nearby beach restaurant serves lunch. *Closed Sept. 15 units. Rates: $145-$185 ($125-$155), two-bedroom deluxe $290 ($230). Tel: 284.494.6979. Fax: 284.494.6980. www.icisvillas.com*

Josiah's Bay Lodging
TAMARIND CLUB HOTEL

Nestled in the hills above remote Josiah's Bay beach is this somewhat rustic retreat with a popular bar and excellent restaurant.

This compact little hideaway is built into the hills high above Josiah's Bay. The pool is sort of the geographical center, with rooms at either end, and the bar and open-air library/common room right alongside the pool. (Swim under the

97

bridge to the swim-up side of the bar). Some units are in a two-story white building with arches framing the verandas and others are in a one-story building on the other side of the pool. The nine units are of various sizes, rustically built, and very simply decorated, but each has a little fridge and all are air-conditioned. The isolated beach is close to a mile downhill but it is pretty easy to catch a ride back up if you don't have a car. The popular restaurant *(see page 87)* turns out excellent cuisine.

9 rooms. Rates (including continental breakfast): $120-$175 ($99-$132). Tel: 284.495-2477. Fax 284.495.2795. www.tamarindclub.com

Beef Island Lodging
SURFSONG VILLA RESORT

These top-of-the-line villas are secluded at the end of a narrow road on a beautiful calm beach on Beef Island. This is a world-class escape with all the tranquility and beauty of the Caribbean and all the modern conveniences of home.

Four delightfully designed and beautifully decorated villas on Well Bay make up this resort. All four villas are distinctive and different and beautifully appointed in every way. They have private balconies or terraces and amazing tropical views. All have deluxe king beds, air-conditioning, fully equipped ultra-modern kitchens, barbecue grills, CD and DVD players, and satellite TV. When you add to this list dedicated phone and fax lines, room safes, robes, and complimentary high-speed Internet access, you have simply superb accommodations. Along with the exceptional setting, Surfsong also offers its guests an informal lounge and honor bar, a Zen Gazebo, a massage pavilion, a library, and a boutique. And the very special people at Surfsong will happily do whatever it takes to make your stay an unforgettable Caribbean experience.

4 villas. Rates: $400-$900 ($250-$650). Entire resort: $2000-$2850. Tel: 284.495.1864. Fax: 284.495.0089. www.surfsong.net

RENTING A VILLA ON TORTOLA

Villas on Tortola run the gamut from simple cottages to spacious houses with state-of-the-art kitchens. Many rentals are located on Beef Island (the location of the airport and connected to Tortola by a little bridge), others are clustered on the far western end of Tortola, and many are scattered all over the island. Purple Pineapple Villa Rentals *(284.495.3100, www.purplepineapple.com)* has a wide selection of villa rentals. Another good bet is Blue Escapes *(512.472.8832, www.blueescapes.com).*

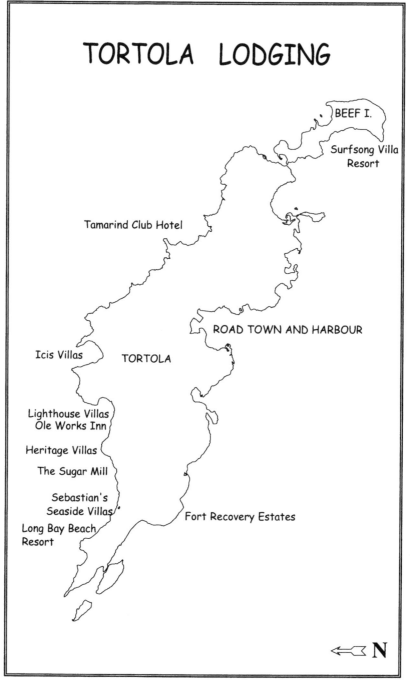

TORTOLA LODGING

BEEF I.

Surfsong Villa Resort

Tamarind Club Hotel

ROAD TOWN AND HARBOUR

Icis Villas

TORTOLA

Lighthouse Villas
Ole Works Inn

Heritage Villas

The Sugar Mill

Sebastian's
Seaside Villas

Long Bay Beach
Resort

Fort Recovery Estates

N

MORE THINGS PEOPLE USUALLY WISH THEY HAD KNOWN SOONER

❑September is exceptionally slow in the BVI and some resorts and restaurants close up. Some stay closed through mid-October. Tortola is the least shut-down island (only a handful of restaurants and resorts actually close) but Virgin Gorda is exceptionally quiet during this time and almost nothing is open on Jost Van Dyke. The advantage of traveling this time of year is that you have the beaches and roads to yourself.

❑When you fly from Puerto Rico to the BVI you are almost always over islands and you really get to see how close everything is. If you are flying on American Eagle, generally the best views are out of the right side of the plane (and the left side going home). You'll get a sense of how these politically separated islands are actually one long string of hills poking out of the sea.

❑You'll see goats, cows, roosters, horses, and an occasional pig on roads and also in town. Contrary to popular opinion, roosters not only crow at dawn but whenever they bloody well feel like it, which is pretty much 24/7 and why some people prefer air-conditioning despite the beautiful breezes.

❑Jost Van Dyke is more crowded on weekends because so many day-trippers come from St. Thomas.

❑To the delight of taxi drivers and the dismay of almost everyone else, from November to April cruise ships disgorge passengers onto Tortola several days a week and they spill into Road Town, Sage Mountain, Skyworld, and Cane Garden Bay. (Check the paper for cruise ship schedules if you want to avoid these crowds.)

CYBER CAFES, THE INTERNET, AND E-MAIL

Even though phone service (expecially long distance) can be difficult to access in the BVI, you can get online at most hotels, either in your room or in the lobby, if you have a laptop. Some hotels also have a computer in the lobby that is available to guests free or for a small fee. In addition, there are a number of cyber cafes. Also, many bars and restaurants have a computer you can log onto. Some of the places you can get connected are listed below.

TORTOLA
West End/Frenchman's Cay
You'll find a row of computer terminals at **Caribbean Jewellers** *(284.495.4137)*.

Road Town
CYM *(284.494.5954)*, located on the marina side of the Mill Mall Complex in downtown Road Town, is a cozy place to come for coffee and juice and to settle down at the computer. **The Pub** *(284.494.2608)*, across the street from Fort Burt just east of Road Town, has several computers just to the right of the bar.

East End/Trellis Bay/Beef Island
Computer terminals are inside the **Trellis Bay Cyber Cafe** *(284.495.2447)*, along with comfortable couches and magazines. Stay for a delicious sandwich on the breezy deck or relax in the hammock. **Fat Hog Bob's** *(284.495.1010)*, at Maya Cove, offers several computer terminals so you can catch up on your e-mail or browse the Internet.

VIRGIN GORDA
Stop by the **Java Connection** *(284.495.7154)* at Leverick Bay or the **Bitter End Yacht Club** *(284.494.2746)* in North Sound for your Internet and e-mail connections. In The Valley head to **Trinket** *(284.495.6562)* at Yacht Harbour.

MUSEUMS AND RUINS

Around the islands you will find a few museums and ruins of forts and a copper mine. Displays are small and informal but often quite interesting.

TORTOLA
Fort Burt
The Dutch constructed this fort to guard the mouth of Road Town Harbour and the British rebuilt it in the late 1600s. Now the remains form the foundation for a bar with a spacious terrace and a stunning view. *Road Town.*

Fort Recovery
Built by the Dutch in 1660, this turreted gun emplacement has walls that are three feet thick. It's the oldest intact structure in the BVI. *Just east of West End.*

Government House
A little museum displays various documents including a handwritten account of one person's experiences during the hurricane of 1924 and signatures of Queen Elizabeth II and the Queen Mother in the Visitor's Book. There are cannonballs, glass bottles, and murals. *Road Town.*

Mount Healthy National Park
Here you'll find the remains of a stone windmill tower, part of a sugar plantation dating from the 18th century. *On the way down to Brewer's Bay.*

VIRGIN GORDA
The Coppermine
Come here to see the remains of a chimney, mine shafts, and a boiler house used by Cornish miners searching for copper in the mid-1800s. *Coppermine Point, The Valley.*

11. VIRGIN GORDA

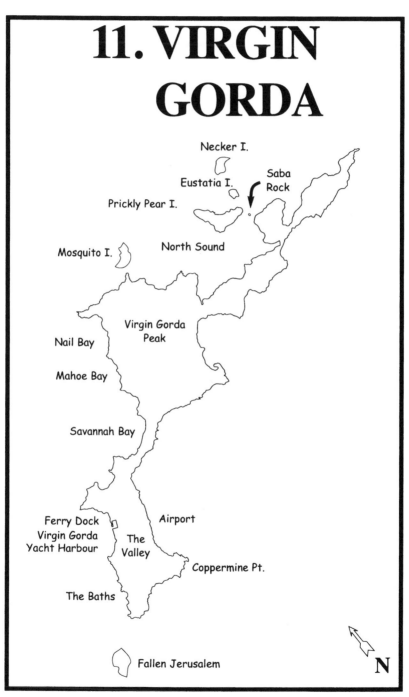

Necker I.

Eustatia I.

Saba Rock

Prickly Pear I.

Mosquito I.

North Sound

Virgin Gorda Peak

Nail Bay

Mahoe Bay

Savannah Bay

Ferry Dock
Virgin Gorda
Yacht Harbour

Airport

The Valley

Coppermine Pt.

The Baths

Fallen Jerusalem

N

VIRGIN GORDA IN A NUTSHELL

Slender Virgin Gorda is 10 miles long and lies seven miles east of Tortola. Only about 3,000 people live there, but it's the second most populated British Virgin Island. A big mountain in the middle divides the island into two separate destinations: The Valley and North Sound. These two areas are somewhat isolated from each other and geographically dissimilar, and visiting these two places are completely different experiences.

The Valley

The southern end of Virgin Gorda, referred to as The Valley or Spanish Town, is rather flat and strewn with giant boulders. The famous Baths are here, as are several other small and lovely beaches. You'll also find a luxury resort, villa rentals and villa rental complexes, restaurants and bars and, at the Virgin Gorda Yacht Harbour, a small cluster of shops. This part of Virgin Gorda is fairly compact, with places to go and stay within a few easy minutes of each other. Just north of The Valley, along the western shore of the mountain that divides the island, there is an additional hotel and several villa rental complexes connected by a road to The Valley. When you want to go anywhere in this part of Virgin Gorda, you walk or drive or taxi across land, the way you do on most islands.

North Sound

An extremely steep road leads up over the top of Virgin Gorda's mountain and drops precipitously down to North Sound. Here, the long and curvy northern shore of Virgin Gorda, along with the shores of Mosquito and Prickly Pear Islands, almost completely encircles the remarkable North Sound, one of the world's most protected sounds.

Resorts are scattered around the hilly rim of North Sound. With the exception of one hotel and villa complex, these resorts are accessible only by boat. A handful of restaurants and little shops also are scattered along the shores and almost all of these, too, are not reachable by road. To get almost anywhere in North Sound, instead of traveling across land you travel back and forth across water, either via water taxi or your own little boat. It can be delightful to experience life without cars.

PART 1: THE VALLEY

Note: This chapter on Virgin Gorda is divided into two sections: The Valley, which begins here, and North Sound, which begins on page 121.

WHAT YOU CAN DO IN THE VALLEY

You can rent a villa or stay in a luxury resort or a condo or a simple cottage. Head to the The Baths and frolic among the boulders and hike or snorkel to several other nearby boulder-filled beaches. Take a picnic to Coppermine Point, a ruin of a copper mine on a windswept rocky point. Hike to the top of Gorda Peak. Rent a little powerboat for a day of exploring or take a boat trip to a great snorkel spot. Then catch your breath and relax at one of the area's mostly casual but delightful restaurants.

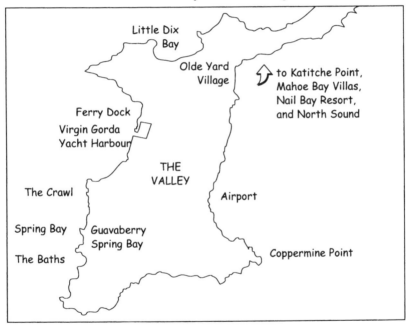

GETTING TO THE VALLEY FROM NEARBY ISLANDS OR NORTH SOUND

You can reach The Valley on Virgin Gorda by public ferry from Road Town on Tortola or Trellis Bay on Beef Island or Charlotte Amalie on St. Thomas *(see Appendix for ferry schedules on page 138)*. From Virgin Gorda's North Sound, you can drive or taxi from Leverick Bay or Gun Creek. For information on arriving from the U.S. or U.K. see page 135.

EXPLORING THE VALLEY

The whole southern end of Virgin Gorda is strewn with giant, smooth-sided boulders. On land, they form remarkable natural sculptures. In the water, they create dramatic pools and secret grottoes. The Baths, Virgin Gorda's most famous landmark, is a stunning showcase for these boulder clusters but you will see them at other beaches as well.

The Virgin Gorda Yacht Harbour is the "hub" of The Valley. Beaches are to the south and north, along the western edge of the island. Coppermine Point is on the southeastern tip of Virgin Gorda. The Baths and other beaches south of Yacht Harbour, the snorkeling areas, and Coppermine Point are all part of the BVI National Parks Trust, a system of protected water and land areas. Please respect signs and don't leave anything behind but your footprints.

Renting a jeep or hiring a taxi

You can rent a car or jeep for $50-$60 a day from **L & S Jeep Rental and Taxi** *(284.495.5297)*, **Mahogany Car Rentals and Taxi** *(284.495.5469)*, or **Speedy's** *(284.495.5240)*. You can usually find a taxi at the ferry dock or at the Taxi Stand in the parking lot south of the Yacht Harbour from these same three outfits. To be picked up, for either a taxi or a car rental, just call. Taxis vary from brightly striped, canopied, open "safari buses" to jeep-type vehicles to regular sedans. The fare to anywhere from anywhere in The Valley (Savannah Bay and south) is $2 to $4 per person. Drivers are happy to drop you at the beach and pick you up later. It's $20 for up to four people to Nail Bay or Gun Creek or Leverick Bay. A two hour island tour is about $45 for two people.

SHORTCUT FROM THE FERRIES TO THE YACHT HARBOUR

Public ferries arrive just north of the Virgin Gorda Yacht Harbour. Taxis meet the ferries and friendly drivers will take you anywhere but if you want to see the Yacht Harbour first, you can easily walk. Go past the ferry terminal, turn right into the parking lot, and head toward the large field bordered by a chain-link fence (don't worry, it's public property). You'll see a path that leads from an opening in the fence. Follow it and in a minute or two you'll be right at Yacht Harbour.

VISITING THE BATHS, OTHER BEACHES, AND COPPERMINE POINT

THE BATHS, DEVIL'S BAY, SPRING BAY, THE CRAWL, LITTLE TRUNK BAY, AND BIG TRUNK BAY

Virgin Gorda's southwest shore is laced with one white sandy crescent of beach after another, each separated by clusters of giant rocky boulders. The scenery here is simply stunning: glistening sand, water in a thousand shades of blue, shapely islands in the distance. Narrow and often hilly walking paths connect the beaches but it is also possible to snorkle from beach to beach when the water is calm. These are superb beaches for swimming and snorkeling. The water is usually calm and always extraordinarily clear.

The Baths. This is Virgin Gorda's most celebrated landmark and, along with The Crawl, is one of the best spots to experience swimming in the pools and grottoes created by the boulders. The Baths is extremely popular but still definitely worth a visit. To avoid the crowds come early or late in the day. The path, which takes about 10 minutes to walk, starts at the circle where you park your car. It's clearly etched into the ground and drops gently, curving around giant boulders. At the beach, you'll find the Poor Man's Bar, a good stop for cold drinks, hot dogs, and sandwiches, plus T-shirts and rental snorkel gear. There are lockers for rent, public restrooms, and a tiny gift shop open whimsical hours. *$3 per person fee*

Devil's Bay. It's just south of The Baths and the most appealing and adventurous route starts at The Baths. Head to the south end of the beach and look for the sign and the narrow space at the bottom of two boulders. Stoop down and head through the space. Be prepared to, as the sign says, "crawl, climb ladders, and wade through water" to get to the next beach. This approach to Devil's Bay takes about 20 minutes. You can come back the way you came or take the land path back from Devil's Bay to the parking circle. You can also start with the land path (it's about a 15-minute walk) and make this trip in reverse; on calm days you can also snorkel from one beach to the other.

Spring Bay. Actually two beaches separated by a few rocks, this is the next beach north of The Baths and far less crowded. A sign marks the spot.

The Crawl. Just north of Spring Bay is this remarkable natural pool formed by giant boulders. The water is extra calm and shallow here and this is a great place for novice snorkelers to practice. A sign marks the entrance to the road leading to the parking lot. From there it's a five-minute walk to the beach. Or you can follow the narrow curvy and hilly path from Spring Bay or Little Trunk Bay.

Little Trunk Bay and Big Trunk Bay. These are the next two beaches north of The Crawl and are connected by little paths (to each other and from The Crawl) but not accessible from the road.

SAVANNAH BAY BEACHES AND POND BAY BEACH

When you are in the mood for a fabulous stretch of beach that is also often deserted, head to the Savannah Bay Beaches and Pond Bay Beach, which are an easy five-minute drive north of the Virgin Gorda Yacht Harbour. Savannah Bay Beach is over half a mile long. Pond Bay Beach and Little Savannah Bay Beach are smaller beaches. The sand here is stunningly white, the waters multihued, and the reef makes anchorages difficult so few people approach from the water. To get to **Savannah Bay Beach,** go past the Olde Yard Village and then over a hill and then look for a turnoff on the left just when the road flattens out. (There's a sign there but it's facing the other way.) Stop in the parking area on the right. Then walk to the turnoff and follow the path to the beach. To get to **Little Savannah Bay Beach,** follow the path at the south end of Savannah Bay Beach. There is a path from the road to **Pond Bay Beach** but it is difficult to see. Drive past the Savannah Bay entrance and you should see the path on the left just before you get to the left turn to Nail Bay. Park along the roadside.

COPPERMINE POINT

Coppermine Point is a rocky spit of land facing west and the prevailing winds stir up the surf. Come here for a great view of crashing waves and to walk among the ruins of an old copper mine. To get there, turn right out of the Yacht Harbour parking lot and take the first left after the round-about and drive until this road ends at a "T." Turn right and stay on this road to the end. The road can be very bouncy and you may feel lost, but stick with it for 10 minutes and you'll arrive.

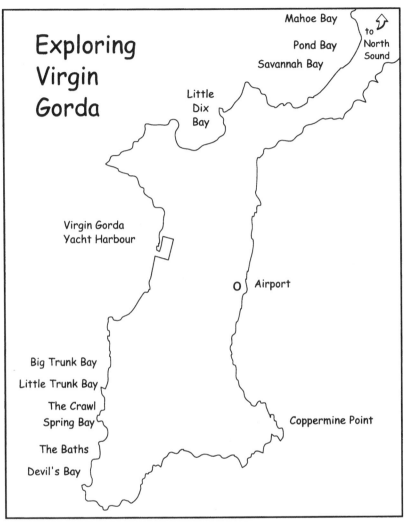

Exploring Virgin Gorda

Mahoe Bay
Pond Bay
Savannah Bay
to North Sound
Little Dix Bay
Virgin Gorda Yacht Harbour
Airport
Big Trunk Bay
Little Trunk Bay
The Crawl
Spring Bay
The Baths
Devil's Bay
Coppermine Point

SNORKELING AND DIVING FROM THE VALLEY

All beaches in The Valley have good snorkeling. If you need equipment (mask, fins, snorkel), you can sometimes rent it from your hotel or you can rent it at The Baths or you can rent or buy equipment from **DIVE BVI** *(284.495.5513)* at Virgin Gorda Yacht Harbour. Divers can call Dive BVI for half-day and full-day diving trips, night dives, and resort courses. If you want to go on a boat trip that includes a bit of snorkeling, see page 111.

GREAT THINGS TO DO ON VIRGIN GORDA

Enjoy the wonderful lunch buffet at Little Dix Resort *(284.495.5555)*. Seating is under a stunning arch that frames a gorgeous view. The cuisine is a delight, too. Plates and plates of composed salads; burgers, dogs, and various entrees; plus fruits, cheeses, and a devilish collection of tasty desserts.

Rent a dinghy and explore North Sound. You can spend the day putt-putting about or you can snorkel over the side or you can just drift about and take in the scenery.

Go floating. Get on one of those yellow or blue floats and just lie there, letting the water carry you about. It's so relaxing. If you are into decadent snorkeling bring your mask, hang your head over the end of the float, and gaze underwater.

Head to Biras Creek Resort for a sweeping sunset view over cocktails and an elegant dinner. Call ahead *(284.494.3555)* and they'll pick you up free at Gun Creek.

Walk around the Virgin Gorda Yacht Harbour. Take a look at all the sailboats and motor yachts.

Treat yourself to a treatment at the Spa at Little Dix Resort *(284.495.5555)*. It's one of the best spas in the Caribbean and the setting is stunning.

Stop by the Mine Shaft Cafe at sunset time. You'll see one of the world's great views. Stay for a romantic, casual meal under the stars. Come early and play a game of miniature golf on the rustic course.

GREAT BOAT TRIPS AND BOAT RENTALS IN THE VALLEY

There are several great cruises available that will take you on a snorkeling adventure or off to another island. On a calm day it's also quite easy and a lot of fun to rent a little boat and go to The Baths and other beaches.

CAPTAINED BOAT TRIPS FROM THE VALLEY
Let someone else do the driving and sit back and enjoy the remarkable views from the water when you take one of these cruises. Choose a sail boat or a powerboat and pick a planned itinerary or create your own!

Spirit of Anegada *(284.499.0901, www.spiritofanegada.com)*, based at the Yacht Harbour, offers daily sailing trips on a 44' gaff-rigged schooner, the *Spirit of Anegada*. The captain usually sails to uninhabited islands for some excellent snorkeling. The cost is $85 per person (minimum 4 people, maximum 10). The *Spirit of Anegada* is also available for half-day trips for $50 per person including beverages or for private charter to almost anywhere for $625 a day or $395 a half day, and also ask about their sunset cruise.

Double "D" Charters *(284.499.2479)* has a great round trip to Anegada that leaves from the Virgin Gorda Yacht Harbour on Thursdays or almost any day. Their 42' cabin cruiser leaves at 9 am and returns around 5 pm. The rate is $95 per person (there's a six-person minimum). Add on an additional $35 per person for ground transportation on Anegada and a lobster lunch at the Big Bamboo on Loblolly Bay. Also check out the cruise opportunities on their 50' sailboat.

Euphoric Cruises *(284.495.5542)* has a 28' Bertram powerboat that is available for day trips with a captain. The boat leaves from Virgin Gorda Yacht Harbour and heads to your choice of island(s), weather permitting. Cost is $750 for a full day; $500 a half day. You can also go on their larger 36' Riviera for $1,100 a day or $750 a half day.

RENTING YOUR OWN LITTLE BOAT
Euphoric Cruises *(284.495.5542)*, at Virgin Gorda Yacht Harbour, features 21' and 26' Robalos which you can take out for the day. The fee for the smaller boats is $250 and for the larger, $350, plus gas.

Power Boat Rentals, Ltd. *(284.495.5542)*. At Virgin Gorda Yacht Harbour, Ash Harrigan offers Seafox 210's, all with biminis, vhf radio, stepladder, and anchor. Rates are $250 per day. Call for weekly rates. They'll deliver boats to (or pick you up in) Virgin Gorda and also Road Town and Trellis Bay in Tortola.

WANT TO GO TO ANEGADA ON YOUR OWN?

Smith's Ferry *(284.494.4454, 284.494.2355)* offers round-trip ferry service by reservation only. Once you're on Anegada, you're on your own. Departure times give you the longest possible day trip. The boat leaves The Valley ferry dock at 7:30 am. It leaves Anegada at 5 pm. Round trip is $50 ($35 for children).

GREAT TRAILS FROM THE VALLEY

The BVI National Parks Trust maintains many parks and protected areas throughout the BVI, including The Baths, adjacent north and south beaches, and Gorda Peak National Park. Trails and picnic spots abound.

GORDA PEAK NATIONAL PARK

This 265-acre park sits atop the highest area of Virgin Gorda (1,359'). The south and north entrances are reachable from the main road between The Valley and North Sound. Small entrance signs and access are on the west side of the road. Here you will find fairly strenuous trails, a lookout tower, and picnic tables. The dense vegetation includes stately mahogany trees and exotic, colorful orchids.

DEVIL'S BAY AND STONEY BAY

Inland and coastal trails lead from The Baths to Devil's Bay, where you will find calm waters and good snorkeling. From Devil's Bay a trail goes to Stoney Bay.

A GLORIOUS SPA

The Spa at Little Dix Bay *(284.495.5555)* is perched high on a hill between sea and bay. Gracious walkways lead through tropical foliage to serene therapy rooms and showcase magnificent Caribbean views. The spa offers just about any treatment you might imagine and some you never would. From a Mango Pineapple Sugar Scrub, to a Lemon Grass Spice Wrap, to more conventional facials and massages, the staff, the setting, and the scenery cannot be beat. There's even a special room for couples' treatments.

GREAT SHOPPING IN THE VALLEY

Shopping in The Valley is limited but interesting. The Virgin Gorda Yacht Harbour has two little collections of shops, one on either side of the main parking lot. The BVI Tourist Board has an office here well stocked with maps, brochures, and menus. Shops are also located at the entrance to The Baths and at Little Dix Bay Resort (see page 114).

VIRGIN GORDA YACHT HARBOUR SHOPPING

Blue Banana *(284.495.6633)* features an appealing variety of beautiful and sophisticated items. Come here for scrunchies, sarongs, candles, aromatherapy, incense, pottery, bathing suits, beach bags, jewelry, colorful cotton pants and tops, note cards, and fancy sun hats.

Buck's Food Market *(284.495.5423)* is Virgin Gorda's primary supermarket, and you'll find fresh, canned, and frozen foods.

DIVE BVI *(284.495.5513)* carries assorted T-shirts, sunglasses, books, and sportswear as well as diving and snorkel equipment (including on-the-spot prescription masks). They also offer dives and instruction.

Kaunda's Kysy Tropix *(284.495.5636)* is the place to come for a great selection of music CDs—reggae, steel bands, rock, top 40s, etc. Also, you can bring your film here for quick processing. They pierce ears, too!

Margo's Jewelry Boutique *(284.495.5237)* showcases handcrafted gold and silver pieces of jewelry, carved wood sculptures, and a few dresses and purses.

Nauti-Virgin Boutique *(284.495.5428)* is a good source for comfortable island wear: gauzy island skirts and colorful T-shirts, shorts, hats, purses, and more.

Ocean Delight Ice Cream Parlour *(284.495.54540)*, hidden behind the Wine Cellar, scoops up icy cold treats in assorted flavors.

Thee Artistic Gallery *(284.495.5104)* displays 14K gold and silver jewelry, books, colorful maps, wind chimes, and watercolors by local artists.

Virgin Gorda Craft Shop *(284.495.5137)* is tucked back in the corner and easy to miss but be sure to stop here for wonderful locally made items.

Wine Cellar and Bakery *(284.495.5250)* carries oven-fresh French bread plus pastries, sodas, wines, and bottled liquor, and, on season, sandwiches.

SHOPPING ELSEWHERE IN THE VALLEY

Caribbean Gift Shop #1 *(284.495.5914)* is located in the pastel blue gingerbread-trimmed cottage at the entrance to The Baths and built around a boulder (it sticks up out of the middle of the floor). Come here for a large display of original handmade silver bracelets and money clips, toe rings, books on the Caribbean, and an enormous T-shirt collection.

Caribbean Two *(284.495.6288)*, sister shop to the above, is in the row of shops on the walkway. It's tiny but you'll find pretty sundresses, sarongs, jewelry, T-shirts, handbags, beach bags, hats, and beach cover-ups.

Little Dix Pavilion Gift Shop *(284.495.5555)*, at Little Dix Resort, caters to the well-heeled, and is an excellent shopper's destination. Look for designer bathing suits, fashionable beach cover-ups, upscale men's and women's resortwear including pants and tops and shirts and skirts, and fancy sandals. There's also a selection of local pottery and artwork, a collection of books on the Caribbean, some unusually artistic picture frames, and plenty of Little Dix logo items, from comfortable T-shirts to hats, beach towels, and bar glasses. If you are searching for a current copy of *The New York Times*, the *Wall Street Journal*, a current news magazine, or even a new paperback, this is the place to come.

A COW STORY

Those grates made of round steel bars that you occasionally drive over, such as the one at the car entrance to the Virgin Gorda Yacht Harbour, are designed to keep out hoofed animals like goats and cows (the animals lose their footing on the bars).

However, cows are smart. Hang around the Yacht Harbour's parking lot for a few minutes and you are bound to see a large cow shoulder her way, effortlessly and without missing a beat, right through the people gate (no round steel bars on the ground here!), as she heads toward wherever it is she is going.

THE VALLEY'S GREAT RESTAURANTS AND BARS

There are a number of excellent restaurants in Virgin Gorda's Valley area. Don't be alarmed if you are the only customer. In the U.S. this could mean the restaurant is awful. In the BVI it indicates nothing. Virgin Gorda has relatively few visitors so sometimes a restaurant serves very few meals in a day. The food will still be delicious and the staff will be delighted you dropped by. Be sure also to check out the restaurant section for Virgin Gorda's North Sound (see page 127). If you don't want to make this drive at night, take a taxi; or you might want to head to North Sound for a wonderful lunchtime adventure.

Chez Bamboo *(284.495.5752)*, just north of the Yacht Harbour, features a delightfully romantic garden setting: tables surrounded by lush plants, a welcoming bar, tiny twinkling lights, and tropical breezes. More tables are inside, along with some interesting murals, a deep blue ceiling, and sparkles. The menu is eclectic. Good appetizers include shrimp jicama spring rolls, steamed mussels, and an andouille pizza. Cajun barbecued shrimp, steak New Orleans, and lobster curry are tasty entree choices. End the evening with hot apple crisp or the retro pineapple upside-down cake for two. *D $$-$$$*

Dog and Dolphin Bar and Restaurant *(284.494.8000)*, at Nail Bay, is high up the hill with stunning views of sea and neighboring islands. This very casual spot is nestled against a free-form swimming pool with a swim-up bar and surrounded by vibrant clusters of bougainvillea. Dine at the bar or at little bistro tables open to the breezes. For dinner choose grilled chicken stuffed with goat cheese, grouper filet with mustard sauce, or barbecued spareribs. The lunch menu features burgers, conch fritters, sandwiches, and salads. Rotis here are great. This is a bit out of the way for dinner if you are staying in the Valley but it's a lovely lunchtime stop and if you dine here you can use the pool. *LD $$*

Flying Iguana *(284.495.5277)* should not be missed! Tables are on a small porch and the decor is ultracasual, but the chef pays exquisite attention to what goes on the plate. Fine lunch choices are the beautifully prepared hamburger, the BLT (in a pita), the outstanding lobster fritters (available as an appetizer at night), and the club sandwich. In the evening, try the Duck by Puck (he's the owner), the fisherman's catch, and the curried coconut shrimp or opt for the Chinese selections: ginger chicken, sweet and sour pork, shrimp chow mein, and more. Pancakes and various egg dishes are served in the morning. *BLD $-$$*

Giorgio's Table *(284.495.5684)* is a 10-minute drive north of Yacht Harbour on Mahoe Bay (take a left just north of Savannah Bay and prepare for a very steep drop). It's a classy-looking restaurant set right at the water's edge and floor-to-ceiling glass doors open and close to regulate the breezes. This is a peaceful place to come for lunch and have a pizza and a salad. For dinner, you can choose one of the many ravioli specials, other Italian dishes, or steak. Dinner, especially if you have an appetizer or soup, can be astonishingly expensive. *LD $$$*

Little Dix Resort's Pavilion *(284.495.5555)*, in a stunning open-air setting with a dramatic view, is a terrific place to come for any meal, day or night. Dinner here is a la carte, except for the lavish Monday night buffet. Breakfast and lunch, which are served buffet-style but elegantly, are outstanding. At lunch, which is a truly relaxing experience, two large tables are filled with a tempting array of composed salads, platters of cheeses, bowls of fresh fruits, and assorted breads. Head to the grill for excellent fish, great hamburgers and hot dogs, and other hot entrees. Then linger with a sampling from the table of tempting sweets. The lunch buffet is $25. Breakfast is $18. *Long pants and collared shirts required for men after sunset. Reservations a must for dinner. BLD $$$*

Little Dix Resort's Sugar Mill *(284.495.5555)* will capture your heart. It is sophisticated and elegant and the perfect choice for a truly romantic evening. Tables look out to tranquil waters, Caribbean breezes caress, and the lighting is so low and the service so seamless that you forget anyone else is around. Start with the seared tuna carpaccio or a mixed satay with spicy peanut sauce. Then dine on garlic shrimps tagliatelle, charbroiled Kobe beef flank steak, or pan-seared red snapper fillet. *No children under 12. Long pants and collared shirts required for men. Reservations a must. D $$$*

Mad Dog *(284.495.5830)* features hot dogs, BLTs, tuna sandwiches, cold beer, and their real claim to fame, frozen Pina Coladas. This tiny and very casual open-air bar can be found tucked among the sea grapes just before the parking circle for The Baths. *Open 10 am-7 pm. L $*

Mine Shaft Cafe *(284.495.5260)*, perched atop a hill, shows off superb scenery. Views from the sunken bar and inside tables are awesome but the view from the deck is even better. You'll see unbelievably brilliant sunsets and at night a billion stars and the lights of Tortola twinkling across the channel! It's a casual place with casual fare to match: nachos, burgers, steak sandwiches, wings, ribs, and rotis. You'll find it on the road to Coppermine Point. *LD $*

Rock Cafe *(284.495.5482)* has three levels of outdoor dining decks tucked in between giant boulders, tropical foliage, and exotic trees. Tables are hidden here and there (one table has a private deck all to itself) and water trickles gently down a waterfall. Italian cuisine is the specialty here. Try the spaghetti primavera, tagliatelle al salmone in a vodka/pink sauce, or the penne caprese (served the traditional Italian way, at room temperature). Save room for the mango cheesecake and the chocolate mousse, which is homemade and the house specialty. Stick around for entertainment late into the night at Sam's Piano Bar *(see below)*. There's also a late night menu of pizzas and snacks. *D $$*

BARS & NIGHTLIFE IN THE VALLEY

There's usually something happening every night but the exact schedule of who is playing where and when is in a state of constant flux. When you are on island, check out the Limin' Times *for the current schedule. Also look for posters pasted on telephone poles and on various walls around the Virgin Gorda Yacht Harbour, especially near the Bath and Turtle.*

The Bath and Turtle *(284.495.5239)* draws crowds Wednesday nights to listen and dance to live local bands. The bar is popular almost anytime day or night.

Chez Bamboo *(284.495.5752)* has a large bar in an outdoor courtyard and features a live band on Fridays.

Dockside Bar & Grill *(284.495.6663)* is built out over the water (from the Rock Cafe, drive west) and is a casual place to enjoy simple food, to hang out, and to watch sunsets.

Flying Iguana *(284.495.5277)* is the locale for the popular band Profile on Tuesday evenings.

Little Dix Resort *(284.495.5555)* features entertainment every evening but Sunday. Enjoy specialty frozen drinks or original martinis in the open-air bar and lounge and dance the night away.

Mine Shaft Cafe and Nightclub *(284.495.5260)* is the place to come for great full-moon parties.

Sam's Piano Bar at the Rock Cafe *(284.495.5482)* is the hottest nightspot on Virgin Gorda. Six nights a week there's live entertainment with something for everyone, from rock to oldies to jazz, reggae, and rhythm and blues. Take a seat around the piano bar or settle into the 1950s-style chairs or chill out in a cozy alcove in this large and dimly lit and appealing nightclub. *8 pm-midnight Sun.-Tues. and also Thurs.-Fri. (closed Wed.); 8 pm-2 am Sat.*

THE VALLEY'S GREAT PLACES TO STAY

In The Valley on Virgin Gorda there are a variety of accommodations. You can choose to stay at a luxury resort, a condo complex, or a comfortable little cottage, or you can rent one of the many wonderful villas here. To check out the resorts on Virgin Gorda's North Sound, see page 130.

Rates are per night for two people on season (off season in parentheses), without meals and without 7% government tax and 10%-12% service charge.

GUAVABERRY SPRING BAY VACATION HOMES

When you want the comfort of having a kitchen, whether you want a simple cottage or a fancy villa with a pool, check into charming Guavaberry.

Guavaberry's cottages and villas are about a mile-and-a-half south of Yacht Harbor and just north of The Baths and are on or within walking distance of lovely Spring Bay Beach. All units are fully equipped and the living is easy here. The hexagonal wooden cottages are scattered in the hills and hover at treetop level, many with great views of neighboring islands. These simple one- and two-bedroom units have separate living/dining areas, compact but complete kitchens, and comfortable decks. The cottages are beautifully positioned to capture the breezes and one wakes to a songbird serenade.

The wonderful collection of private villas, ranging in size from a studio to five bedrooms, offers something for everyone. All have views, whether right on the beach, or built into the boulders, or poking out of tropical greenery. Kitchens are fully equipped, right down to the little details, like garlic presses. Some villas have stunning private swimming pools and some have air-conditioned bedrooms. One has a tennis court. All are comfortably and stylishly furnished and a few are extremely elegant, with fancy decor and state-of-the-art kitchens. Some villas are much more secluded than others.

Daily maid service is provided for both cottages and villas. A delightfully well-stocked little commissary carries everything from peanut butter to frozen spinach to rental snorkel equipment to beer, wine, and champagne. If you want fresh bread put your order in by 3 pm. There are safes in all units, no TVs, and phones in the villas only. Management is truly outstanding.

18 cottages, 16 villas. Rates (plus 7% tax but no additional service charge): one-bedroom cottage $215 ($140), two-bedroom cottage $280 ($190); villas $2,350 ($1,750) to $7,620 ($5,500) per week. No credit cards. Tel: 284.495.5227. Fax: 284.495.5283. www.guavaberryspringbay.com

118

KATITCHE POINT GREATHOUSE
This fabulous villa, one of the finest in all of the Caribbean, surrounds you with luxury, shimmering seas, and absolutely spectacular views.

A stunning hilltop setting, five exquisitely decorated suites, spacious living areas inside and out, a gorgeous disappearing-edge pool, a Viking kitchen, Bose sound, breakfast prepared for you, a path down to the beach and snorkeling...what more could you want? Perhaps a private chef for dinner? Just ask. Almost anything can be arranged. This is one magnificent villa. Inquire about Salt Spring and Red Rock villas if Katitche Point is booked.
A member of the Small Luxury Hotels of the World. Available for up to 10 people. Weekly rates: 5 suites $22,000 ($16,000); 4 suites $19,300 ($13,700); Just the two of you $6,390; plus 12% service charge. Res: 284.495.6274 or rentals@katitchepoint.de. www.katitchepoint.com

LITTLE DIX BAY
This luxury resort, a Rosewood property, runs along the crescent-shaped shore of one of Virgin Gorda's calmest and prettiest bays.

Little Dix Bay is an upscale, elegant retreat just north of town. It's quiet and peaceful here. Despite the fact that this is one of the largest resorts in the BVI, you can feel wonderfully alone. Rooms, all with patios or balconies and air-conditioned, are two or four to a building and scattered over a half-mile of beautifully manicured grounds. Some have great views, and some are hidden among the trees. King beds back up to stunning stone walls, beams run across the ceilings, and bathrooms are roomy with walk-in showers big enough for two. Junior suites are luxurious and extra-spacious, with a large terrace, two walk-in closets, a soaking tub, and an indoor and outdoor shower. Villas have private pools. A luxurious hilltop spa features a curvy plunge pool, nine treatment cottages (including one for couples), and a fantastic menu of services.

The Pavilion restaurant *(see page 116)*, an open-air affair with a stunning view, is the setting for lavish buffet breakfasts and lunches and a la carte dinners. The intimate, al fresco Sugar Mill *(see page 116)* is a romantic dinner choice. The casual Beach Grill serves salads, sandwiches, and grilled items. Head to the long silken beach for a peaceful walk, find yourself a float and relax or look for turtles, snorkel (best at the north end of the beach), hike to Savannah Bay (when you're sure you're lost, you'll suddenly be there), play tennis (seven courts), be dropped at a deserted beach, then dance the evening away. The children's program is superb. Men's evening dress code is collared shirt, slacks, no sandals.
97 units. Rates: $675-$1,100 ($395-$725) plus 10% service charge. Suites, villas more. Res: 800.928.3000. Tel: 284.495.5555. Fax 284.495.5661. www.littledixbay.com

MAHOE BAY VILLAS
Stunning villas, each with its own private pool, face lovely Mahoe Bay.

Nestled between hillside and beach is this wonderful collection of upscale villas. Each one has a private swiming pool and there is a communal tennis court. Villas have from two to five bedrooms, are privately owned and individually furnished, and many can be rented through Virgin Gorda Villa Rentals.
17 villas. Weekly rates: $4,500-$10,800 ($3,200-$8,200) including tax and service charge (higher holidays). Tel: 284.495.7421. Fax: 284.495.7367. www.virgingordabvi.com

NAIL BAY RESORT
Stay in a room or a suite or splurge on a fabulous villa right on the beach or up in the hills at this state-of-the-art resort and villa complex.

The dream of visionary Agit George, Nail Bay Resort is built on 147 acres of steep hillside that sweeps down to three long and slender beaches on the west side of Virgin Gorda, about five miles north of the Valley. Guests rent either condo-like units or privately owned villas that range from comfortably luxurious to breathtakingly fabulous. If you fall in love with Nail Bay, as many do, you can buy land and build your own. Rooms and apartments are in two West Indian-style hillside buildings and look out to stunning views of the sea. All have air-conditioning, TV/VCRs, and kitchenettes or kitchens. Each of the one- to five-bedroom villas is unique. You'll find stunning "disappearing edge" swimming pools, windows that become waterfalls, plunge pools, magnificent stone walls, artistic sculptures and sculptured gardens, futuristic kitchens. Hike the hills; walk the beaches; snorkel; play tennis, bocce, croquet, or horseshoes; or laze in the free-form pool, complete with a waterfall and swim-up bar. If you don't want to cook, try In-Villa Dining or the Dog and Dolphin *(see page 115)*.
35 units, 10 villas. Daily rates: rooms $200-$250 ($155), suites $295-$600 ($220-$390), villas $295-$940 ($220-$655) plus 10% service charge. Tel: 800.871.3551 or 284.495.5452. Fax 284.495.5875. www.nailbay.com

OLDE YARD VILLAGE
Full kitchens and a central location make this a practical and comfortable stop.

Paths lead through bright tropical flowers to these one-, two-, and three-bedroom condos which are in several two-story yellow buildings. This complex is just a few minutes north of The Valley and not far from beaches. The large, free-form swimming pool is a delightful oasis. The poolside restaurant serves breakfast, lunch, and libations. Two tennis courts and a fitness center are here.
20 units. Rates: one-bedroom units $250-$325 ($190-$210), larger units more. Tel: 284.495.5544. Fax: 284.495.5986. www.oldeyardvillage.com

PART 2: NORTH SOUND

Note: This chapter on Virgin Gorda is divided into two sections: North Sound, which begins here, and The Valley, which begins on page 105.

WHAT YOU CAN DO IN NORTH SOUND

You can stay in an elegant resort or a yachting resort or a simple hotel or you can rent a villa. North Sound is "paradise found" for water lovers. This water wonderland is the place to come for almost every possible kind of water sport. Here you can snorkel, swim, sail, windsurf, rent motorboats, and water-ski, or you can learn how to do any of these things. There are also bars, casual eateries, and an elegant restaurant.

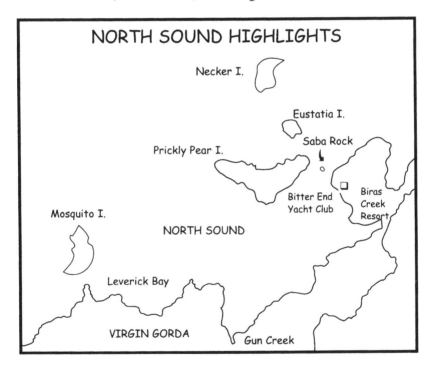

NORTH SOUND HIGHLIGHTS

Necker I.

Eustatia I.

Saba Rock

Prickly Pear I.

Bitter End Yacht Club

Biras Creek Resort

Mosquito I.

NORTH SOUND

Leverick Bay

VIRGIN GORDA

Gun Creek

GETTING TO NORTH SOUND FROM TORTOLA OR THE VALLEY

To get here from Tortola you can take the North Sound Express from Beef Island at the east end of Tortola. It stops at Leverick Bay and Bitter End *(see Appendix for ferry schedules on page 139)*. From The Valley, you can drive or take a taxi to Leverick Bay or Gun Creek.

EXPLORING NORTH SOUND

In North Sound you travel mainly by water and you can take water taxis and ferries to restaurants and beaches. You can also rent your own dinghy and travel to a number of different beaches and unbelievably great snorkeling spots.

Hiring a Water Taxi
You can hire a water taxi at the **Water Sports Center at Leverick Bay** *(284.495.7376)* to take you to Bitter End. The taxi will pick you up at Bitter End for the trip back any time you want before 5 pm. Round trip fare is $25.

Taking a Little Ferry
Free ferries *(see schedule, page 140)* run between Gun Creek and The Bitter End Yacht Club, and there are many boat trips that leave from The Bitter End *(see page 124)*. If you want to dine at Saba Rock, call 284.495.7711 and a ferry will come and pick you up at any other North Sound dock (Leverick Bay, Gun Creek, Biras Creek, Bitter End).

Renting a Dinghy or a Powerboat
The Bitter End Yacht Club *(284.494.2746)* rents Boston Whalers starting at $70 a half day and $85 for a full day. At **Leverick Bay**, the **Water Sports Center** *(284.495.7376)* rents 10' dinghies with 15 hp engines. Rates are $70 a half day, $85 a full day, and $475 a week. If you want something larger, choose one of their Bradleys (17' to 30'). All rates are plus gas and oil.

EXPLORING NORTH SOUND BY DINGHY
North Sound is an absolutely wonderful place to explore in a dinghy. There are deserted beaches to visit and great snorkeling spots to anchor near. You can drift about in very calm water and motor over to restaurants and bars and little shops. For a quiet ride, putter in towards Deep Bay or around the outskirts of Eustatia Sound. Be very careful and go very slowly near Eustatia Sound Reef. The water gets pretty shallow and you don't want to run over and damage any coral. When you feel like lunch or a snack or a beverage, just tie your boat up at one of the many little dinghy docks. You'll find one at Saba Rock, at the Bitter End Yacht Club, at Leverick Bay, at the Fat Virgin at Biras Creek, and the Sand Box on Prickly Pear. Be sure to bring and use sunscreen and some kind of cover-up to protect you from the sun (it can be so breezy and feel so cool when you are out on the water that it is hard to remember that the sun can still burn).

BEACHES AND WATER SPORTS ON NORTH SOUND

There are some nice beaches on North Sound and really great snorkeling spots are practically everywhere. To rent watersports equipment, head to Leverick Bay or the Bitter End Yacht Club.

Beaches

The best beaches are reachable by dinghy. Head to Vixen Point on Prickly Pear for a lovely point of soft white sand and very calm water. The Sand Box restaurant is here. About midway on the west side of Prickly Pear is Honeymoon Beach, a tiny beach that's just about the right size for two. Around to the north (take the passage between Prickly Pear and Saba Rock and then bear west) is a long stretch of beach, which is a lovely stop on a calm day but beware there is no shade. You can dinghy over to the west side of Eustatia Island for a small beach with a nice view of Necker Island or head to the east side of the island to the long beach that looks across to Bitter End. Bitter End has a narrow beach.

Sailboards, Kayaks, Alden Rowing Shells, and Sailboats

Bitter End Yacht Club *(284.494.2746)* has a huge variety of water sports rentals. Come here to rent sailboards, sunfish, lasers, 19' Rhodes, J-24 sailboats, kayaks, Alden Rowing Shells, and more. Rates are $15-$20 per hour. **The Water Sports Center** at Leverick Bay *(284.495.7376)* rents sunfish, Hobi Waves, and two-seater sea kayaks. Instruction is available in water-skiing, sunfishing, and Hobie Cat sailing for no additional charge.

Parasailing and Water-skiing

The Water Sports Center *(284.495.7376)* at Leverick Bay is the place to come for a thrilling parasailing ride for people age 2 to 92! You'll spot turtles and sea rays from 600' up. Rates are $55 for 10 minutes. Water-ski off their competition mastercraft ski boat. Rates are $90 an hour, $60 a half hour. Barefooters use the barefoot boom and wakeboarders try the skylon pylon.

Snorkeling

Head to the reefs all around Eustatia Sound, the reefs on the east and west sides of Eustatia Island, Cactus Reef just off the northwest end of Prickly Pear Island, Honeymoon Beach, Little Trunk Bay south of Mosquito Island, and the windward side of Prickly Pear Island. If you need snorkel equipment, rent it from **The Water Sports Center** *(284.495.7376)* at Leverick Bay for $8 a day or buy it at DIVE BVI *(284.495.7328)*.

123

GREAT CAPTAINED BOAT AND SNORKELING TRIPS FROM NORTH SOUND

Statia Reef Snorkel Trip

Join one of the twice-daily snorkel trips to beautiful Statia Reef on the 40' *Ponce de Leon*, a boat specially designed for snorkeling. The short morning trip, which makes one snorkeling stop, is $10 per person. In the afternoon, the boat makes three snorkeling stops and the cost is $20 per person. Call the Bitter End *(284.494.2746)*.

Powerboat to Anegada

Ride in comfort on the diesel-powered *Corinthian* to Anegada. On Tuesdays or Wednesdays you get a chance to explore the island, go to the beach, snorkel, and have lunch at the Big Bamboo. The boat leaves at 9:30 am and returns about 4 pm. The fare is $85 per person, including lunch. Other days the boat heads to The Baths and Norman Island. Call the Bitter End *(284.494.2746)*.

Cigarette boat to Anegada or around the BVI

The Water Sports Center at Leverick Bay *(284.495.7376)* usually offers full-day trips to Anegada. You go to Loblolly Bay or Cow Wreck Beach. The cost is $650 (10-person maximum).

Sunset Cruise

Take an early evening cruise around North Sound while sipping champagne. The 40' *Ponce de Leon* leaves at 5:30 pm and returns about 7:30 pm, and sometimes a steel band entertains. The cost is $40 per person. Make reservations with the Bitter End *(284.494.2746)*.

Deep-Sea Fishing

Catch tuna, swordfish, wahoo, and more. The **Bitter End** *(284.494.2746)* runs offshore fishing trips on a 26' speedboat. The rate for a half-day is $400. **Captain Dale** *(284.495.7248)* offers half-day and full-day deep-sea fishing charters on his 31' Bertram. Call **Charter Virgin Gorda** *(284.495.7421, cell 284.496.6946, www.chartervirgingorda.com)* for a full-day or a half-day on the *Mahoe Bay*, a comfortable 46' Hatteras designed for deep-sea fishing. The captain can take you to the Sea Mount or to the North Drop or wherever else you choose. Rates are $800 for four hours, $1200 for eight hours, $150 for additional hours.

Sailing to Other Islands

Spice (284.495.7044, or book through Leverick Bay Watersports *284.495.7376),* combines great snorkeling with outstanding sailing. This 51' sloop is perfect for a full or half day of exploring the BVI waters. Cruise to the Baths, Cooper Island, the Dogs, Norman Island, Anegada, or even Jost Van Dyke. Experience extraordinary snorkeling and visit cool little beach bars. Every Thursday the *Spice* heads to Anegada for the day. Full days are $85 and half days are $60 per person. A private charter is $600 (maximum of 8).

Trip to Norman Island

Take this trip down the Sir Francis Drake Channel and snorkel at the famous Caves. The boat leaves every Thursday at 9:30 am and the cost, including a barbecue lunch, is $85 per person. Every Friday the boat heads to Norman Island and a snorkel at the caves with a stop at the Willie T. Call the Bitter End Yacht Club *(284.494.2746).*

Design your own Snorkel Trip

For the best in private snorkel trips, deserted beach adventures, visits to several deserted and non-deserted islands, deep-sea fishing, or a combination of all of these, call Captain Sandy at **Charter Virgin Gorda** *(284.495.7421, cell 284.496.6946, www.chartervirgingorda.com).* You can tailor-make your trip according to what you want to do. The boat, the *Mahoe Bay*, is a 46' Hatteras and is large enough to comfortably accommodate 12 adults and children.

Hitch a Ride with a Dive Boat

DIVE BVI *(284.495.7328)* takes snorkelers along on their afternoon dives. Call to find out where the dive boats are going on a particular day.

HOP ON A SEAPLANE !

Get a great bird's-eye view of your surroundings. You'll see green mountainous islands and waters in an uncountable number of stunning shades of blue. Call Neil Perks at Flight Adventures *(284.495.2311 or 284.499.1456; e-mail: flightadventures@surfbvi.com)* to see if he is up and running. Book a ride on his twin-engine, 3-seat Air Cam Seaplane which was originally designed for a *National Geographic* shoot along the Amazon River. Take the 20-minute introductory flight which goes around Necker Island, Eustatia Reef, and Pajeros Point or head out and about and check out Anegada or Jost Van Dyke from the air. The plane is anchored in front of Prickly Pear Island in North Sound.

SHOPPING IN NORTH SOUND

LEVERICK BAY SHOPPING

Chef's Pantry at Leverick Bay *(284.495.7154)* carries groceries, fresh produce, liquor and beer, canned goods, frozen meats, cheeses, and snacks.

DIVE BVI *(284.495.7328)* sells a variety of swimwear, hats, postcards, colorful T-shirts, collared shirts in bright designs, local artwork including Flukes prints, and island books, and rents and sells snorkel and diving gear.

Palm Tree Gallery *(284.495.7479)* is definitely worth a stop (it's in the back of the plaza, past DIVE BVI). There are many wonderful things to buy here. Look at the lovely selection of jewelry including fish, seashell, and sailboat charms. This is also the place to come for handmade Caribbean batik, art from the BVI and other Caribbean islands, island books, postcards, wind chimes, candles, and appealing decorative boxes.

Pusser's Company Store *(284.495.7369)* carries a large collection of fashionable but comfortable clothing for the whole family, plus all sizes of bottles of their famous rum, as well as souvenirs, postcards, and books.

NORTH SOUND RESORT SHOPPING

Bitter End Emporium *(284.495.2746)* features freshly baked breads and pastries, gourmet items, and canned goods, plus slices of pizza and sodas.

Fat Virgin's Treasure *(284.495.7054)* is at the Biras Creek Resort, right behind the Fat Virgin Cafe. Tie up your dinghy at the dock and spend some time here. You'll find fashionable sunglasses, colorful hats, bathing suits, chic resortwear, local art and pottery, frameable maps, island books, and many items marked with the well-known Biras Creek Resort logo.

Saba Rock Resort Gift Shop *(284.495.7711)* is an elegant stop. Dark wood walls and air-conditioning provide a respite from the sun. Browse through a delightful collection of men's and women's shorts, pants, and shirts; shelves of books; plus watches, sunglasses, rare coins, hats, jewelry, and nautical items.

CARIBBEAN DREAMS

Wish you could pack up Virgin Gorda and bring the island home? You can, with *Caribbean Dreams* by Regine Hodeige and Michael Wissing, a book of glorious photographs and text.

NORTH SOUND'S GREAT RESTAURANTS AND BARS

All of these places are easily reachable by dinghy if you are already in North Sound. If you happen to be coming from The Valley, you can drive directly to the Restaurant at Leverick Bay. For the rest, you will need to catch a ferry (see Appendix for schedules on page 140) or arrrive by dinghy. Some restaurants will send a boat for you free of charge (see individual restaurant descriptions).

Biras Creek Resort *(284.494.3555)* has one of the most romantic dining rooms in the Caribbean. It's in the "Castle," a stunning stonework structure set at the peak of a hill and overlooking both the Caribbean Sea and the calm North Sound. The expansive terrace and al fresco lounge, which face North Sound, are breathtaking settings for an evening cocktail. Come here to catch the ever-changing colors of the sky at sunset and, after dark, watch the twinkling lights on the distant hillsides compete with the stars. Dinner is served by candlelight in several open-air dining rooms. The four-course menu changes nightly and includes several choices for appetizers, a number of main course choices, several desserts, and a cheese board selection. Starters might include cream of sweet potato soup, Caesar salad, and five-spice duck salad. Entrees could be grilled mahi mahi with a chorizo risotto, grilled loin of veal with spinach and a cream of root vegetables, honey-roasted duck breast, and a filet mignon with Bernaise sauce. A vegetarian dish is always offered. Dessert choices might be a chocolate tart with warm chocolate sauce, banana creme brulee, or white chocolate mousse with a mango-lime salsa. The wine list here is exceptional. The prix fixe dinner is $85 per person plus 15% service. Biras Creek will provide complimentary boat transportation from Gun Creek or Bitter End. *Dress is casual elegant (long trousers and collared shirts for men). Reservations for dinner and transportation a must. D $$$*

The Clubhouse at the **Bitter End Yacht Club** *(284.494.2746)* offers casual meals in an open-air dining room and on a terrace near the water. Breakfast, for $17 to $22, includes a buffet of fruits, juices, and pastries plus a choice of eggs, pancakes, or French toast. (On Sunday it's a lavish brunch instead for $29.) Lunch, for $22-$25, is a buffet of salads, plus a choice of entrees such as a hamburger, grilled fish sandwich, or conch fritters. Dinner, for $29 to $55, includes a salad and dessert buffet plus a choice of entrees such as ribs, steaks, fish, or lobster. There's usually a lively beach barbecue on Friday. All prices are plus a 15% service charge. *BLD $$-$$$*

127

Fat Virgin's Cafe *(284.495.7052)*, at Biras Creek Marina (just tie up at the little dinghy dock), is an extremely casual outdoor spot and offers absolutely superb sandwiches and salads all day long. Come here for a great hamburger, a terrific (and very authentic) chicken or vegetable roti, and an excellent tuna salad sandwich on five-grain bread. The menu is the same day and night, except on Friday, when you can also get a full selection of Chinese offerings. *LD (closes 6 pm off season) $$*

Last Stop Bar *(no phone)*, up a little incline just across from the Gun Creek dock and overlooking the water, is a tiny little bar that serves beverages all day long. This is a good stop when you are waiting for a ferry or a taxi. *$*

Restaurant at Leverick Bay *(284.495.7154)*, at Leverick Bay, is actually two places. Upstairs and open to the breezes you'll find a small lounge area and long rectangular bar, plus tables overlooking the water. Good choices for starters are the sweet potato soup and the grilled scallop and parma ham skewers. Then move on to the mahi mahi, pan-seared filet mignon with whiskey-green peppercorn sauce, or Asian chicken breast. At the ultracasual **Jumbies**, tables are on a little terrace facing the beach. Come here for a casual lunch or dinner or afternoon snack. Have a burger or a pizza or wings or shepherd's pie. Don't miss the Friday barbecue. *BLD $$*

Sand Box *(284.495.9122)*, a barefoot beach bar at Vixen Point on Prickly Pear Island, is the place to come for burgers, salads, and sandwiches at lunch and conch chowder, pumpkin soup, grilled sirloin steak, sauteed conch, and swordfish with a spicy Creole sauce for dinner. *Closed days when a small cruise ship is in and closed Aug. and Sept. LD $-$$*

Saba Rock *(284.495.7711)* is on a rock just 200 yards or so from the Bitter End and it's a breezy, waterfront magnet for the yachting crowd who come for Anegada conch fritters, burgers, sandwiches, and the salad bar at lunch and return for the grilled swordfish, mahi mahi, and N.Y. steak at dinner. Ice cream sundaes and banana splits are a big draw, too. Call for free pickup at any North Sound dock. *LD $-$$*

"There is nothing which has yet been contrived by man by which so much happiness is produced as by a good tavern or inn"— or a BVI restaurant or bar.

— logical update of
Dr. Johnson's oft-quoted comment

NIGHTLIFE ON NORTH SOUND

Schedules change all the time so check local papers or look for a copy of the Limin' Times, *which comes out weekly and is very accurate. It's also a good idea to call before you go.*

Biras Creek Resort *(284.494.3555)* presents Calypso singer Mark Morris Tuesday nights, Dennis Brown and his light dancing music Thursday nights, and a great steel band every Saturday night.

Bitter End Yacht Club *(284.494.2746)* gets the crowds on Fridays when local bands entertain.

Leverick Bay *(284.495.7154)* features the sounds of Mark Morris Saturday nights. Catch live reggae on the beach every Tuesday and join in the limbo contest every Friday at the lively barbecue buffet at **Jumbies**, just below the restaurant. The Latitude Stars play Saturday.

Sand Box *(284.495.9122)* is an easy hop from the Bitter End Yacht Club or Biras Creek. Tie up at the little dinghy dock. Local bands entertain Mondays and Wednesdays in season. Closed Aug. to mid-Oct.

Saba Rock *(284.495.7711)* rocks nightly starting at 8 pm. Some nights it's a steel drum band, some nights it's fungi but the crowds are always dancing. Catch the water taxi at Bitter End.

BIRAS CREEK: A GREAT PLACE FOR PEACEFUL COCKTAILS

When you are looking for that "perfect" setting for a quiet cocktail, nothing beats the "Castle" terrace at **Biras Creek Resort** *(284.494.3555)*. It's spectacularly romantic. Although distant islands hide the sun as it slips into the sea, you are high enough to catch the ever-changing colors across the enormous panorama of water, sky, and hills as you gaze across North Sound, watching the sunlight change to nightlight.

NORTH SOUND'S GREAT RESORTS AND VILLAS

Along the shores of Virgin Gorda's North Sound are several great places to stay. Three are accessible only by boat. Few places have room keys but you can lock yourself in at night, if you wish. If you want to check out the resorts in The Valley on Virgin Gorda, see page 118.

Rates are per night for two people on season (off season in parentheses), without meals (unless otherwise stated), and without 7% tax and 10% or 12% service.

BIRAS CREEK RESORT

A romantic, intimate hideaway, and one of five Relais & Chateaux in the Caribbean, this is a true escape, a place to come for isolation and peace.

Biras Creek is a 140-acre resort on a peninsula with the Caribbean Sea on one side and calm North Sound on the other. It is accessible only by boat. Suites are in duplex cottages, many of which are tucked along the rocky ocean's edge. All have private entrances hidden among tropical flowers so you rarely know you are sharing a building. These inviting suites include a cozy sitting area with a coffee maker and little fridge, a separate bedroom, a delightful garden shower open to the sky, a CD player, safe, bikes, and a little patio. The two Grand Suites are outstanding romantic retreats, each with a large and extremely comfortable living room with a veranda, a giant bedroom with its own veranda, and a spacious bathroom with an outdoor shower for two and a soaking tub with a fabulous view. Dinner *(see page 127)* and drinks are served in the "Castle," a splendid stonework structure perched on a hill that straddles the peninsula with knockout views of both the surfy Caribbean sea and tranquil North Sound. Guests gather in the open-air lounge and on the terrace for before-dinner drinks and after dinner, three nights a week, to dance under the stars. Sail-A-Way packages include two nights on a captained yacht. Lunch is a simple affair mostly served at the beach. Do use your voucher at least once for the excellent Fat Virgin Cafe.

This is an incredibly easy place to do nothing or anything. Ride a bike over the long road to the secluded swimming beach or head to the spectacular pool overlooking the ocean, explore North Sound in a dinghy, play tennis or snooker, hike through the woods, be dropped at a deserted beach with a picnic, take a sail to Anegada. Before bed, relax on your patio—the total absence of artificial light makes for extraordinary stargazing.

33 suites. Rates (including meals, use of dinghies, 26' Folk sailing boats, escorted snorkel trips, much more): $980-$1,075 ($615-$775); Grand Suites $1,500 ($885); 2-bedroom suite $1,950 ($1,185) plus 10% service charge. Res: 800.223.1108. Tel: 284.494.3555. Fax: 284.494.3557. www.biras.com.

BITTER END YACHT CLUB

Practically a scheduled stop for charterers (if it's Thursday this must be the Bitter End), this busy marina-cum-resort is a great spot for families and couples who like sailing or who want to learn how.

Accessible only by water, the Bitter End Yacht Club is nestled along the shore overlooking North Sound and Statia Sound and has 100 moorings. The waterfront area is bustling, with boaters coming ashore for provisions, kids taking sailing lessons, couples heading out on dinghies. Beachfront Villas (which are actually built low on a hill overlooking Statia Sound) are cooled by ceiling fans and are very "island-like" with floor-to-ceiling sliding glass doors on two sides, stone walls, and a wide deck, complete with hammock. The air-conditioned North Sound Suites are high on a hill above the pool and look out to the west across North Sound. The beaches aren't top-notch here but you can dinghy to several wonderful ones and there's great snorkeling all over the place. There's also a pool (usually closed September), a fitness trail, and hiking trails.

The real draw here is sailing and learning how to sail. Guests have unlimited use of the resort's outstanding fleet of over 100 day boats, including Hobie waves, Vanguard 15s, Sunfish, Escapes, Optimists, Lasers, Rhodes 19s, J-24s, Mistral Windsurfers, Rowing sculls, Boston Whaler tenders, and ocean kayaks. If you need instruction, just ask one of the water sports staff. The popular Admiral's Package includes all meals, an introductory sailing course (the Nick Trotter Sailing School is located here), daily excursions to other islands and snorkeling trips, and unlimited use of the BEYC fleet. You can also stay overnight on a 30' sailboat even if you have never been on a boat before.
95 units, including 8 "Freedom 30" Yachts. FAP Rates: $735-820 ($590-$715); Admiral's Package rates for 7 nights: $4,095-$5,950 ($3,010-$3,675), plus 11% service charge. Res: 800.872.2392. Tel: 284.494.2746. Fax 284.494.4756. www.beyc.com

LEVERICK BAY RESORT

The small hillside hotel here is a perfect economical stop if you like water sports and want to spend your days exploring North Sound.

Leverick Bay, although tiny, is the largest "settlement" at the north end of Virgin Gorda and consists of a marina, restaurant, bar, day spa, and a cluster of shops. Simple but nicely decorated hotel rooms run along a hillside and the views are terrific from the rooms and balconies. There are also suites with full kitchens. You can watch the activity at the little dock down below or rent a dinghy, catch a day sail, water-ski, or parasail. There's a tiny sliver of beach and a small pool.
14 rooms. Rates $149 (off season $119); suites more. Res: 800.848.7081. Tel: 284.495.7421. Fax 284.495.7367. www.leverickbay.com

SABA ROCK RESORT

There's no beach here, but you can dinghy to one, the rooms are comfortable and contemporary, and great snorkeling is everywhere.

This could be the tiniest resort property in the Caribbean. It's built on what was once just a spit of a rock, 200 yards or so from the Bitter End Yacht Club. In fact long-time visitors to the BVI who used to pull their dinghy up to that rickety little dock and bar on the original Saba Rock will not believe their eyes. What was once barely a bar is now an eight-room resort with a large gift shop plus a popular restaurant and watering hole. The large, open-air restaurant and bar stretches along the entire south side of the islet. Rooms and two-bedrooms suites are above and one room is by itself on the north side of the islet. All are surprisingly spacious and very contemporary, with cathedral ceilings, attractive fabrics and furnishings, air-conditioning and ceiling fans, dish TV, and small balconies. Instead of a beach, there is a large sandy area with lounge chairs and hammocks and a path through beautifully manicured gardens. You can rent dinghies and take the free ferry to the Bitter End Yacht Club.
8 units. Rates $150-$400 ($150-$400). Closed Sept. Res: 284.495.9966. Tel: 284.495.7711. Fax: 284.495.7373. www.sabarock.com

VIRGIN GORDA VILLA RENTALS

Choose a simple cottage or a fancy house overlooking North Sound.

Leverick Bay is the only place on North Sound with a large number of rental villas. They range in size from one to five bedrooms and some have pools. *29 villas. Weekly rates: $1,400-$8,400 ($1,000-$4,400) including tax and service charge (higher holidays). Tel: 284.495.7421. Fax: 284.495.7367. www.virgingordabvi.com*

A WORD ABOUT BVI LODGING

Bear in mind that BVI lodging is in scale with the BVI. Resorts here are smaller. A single full-service resort in the U.S. might have 1,000 rooms and, in fact, there are fewer than 1,000 hotel rooms in all of the British Virgin Islands. Also, in the BVI, as on most islands, many "expected" services such as room service or dry cleaning usually aren't available (there is only one dry cleaner in the BVI). The trade-off for this lack of "services" is an extraordinary peace and quiet, an incredibly relaxed pace, and truly empty beaches.

MORE DRIVING HINTS

ROUNDABOUTS

You'll encounter round-a-bouts if you drive on Virgin Gorda or Tortola. They are places where four or five roads run into a circle. The driver enters the circle, drives along part of it, and then exits on the road of choice. The only people who go full circle are those who want to go back the way they came or those who've spent their lives going around in circles. Remember to turn left into the circle, to turn left out of the circle, and to drive clockwise while in the circle.

BEWARE THE MULE

There is sometimes a mule tied to a tree on the dirt road that lies between BVI Boardsailing and De Loose Mongoose on Tortola's Trellis Bay. On occasion, he tangles his rope around the trees on one side of the road and then heads over to the other side of the road to munch on tree leaves. Sometimes the rope becomes tightly stretched across the road about three feet above the ground, successfully halting all traffic. If this happens to you and you happen to be the only car in sight, hop out of whatever side of the car he's not on (mules have big teeth and like to bite) and give the rope a good tug. You should be able to get enough slack to get the rope to the ground so you can drive across it. Or you can head back to De Loose Mongoose and have another beer.

ROAD SIGNS

Although road signs have been posted around the islands for several years, road names are almost as unfamiliar to the residents as they are to you. For years, locals have used landmarks for directions so it really helps to know that on Virgin Gorda, everything is either in The Valley or in North Sound, and on Tortola, places are always near a bay (Sea Cow's or Long or Apple and so on).

PRACTICAL INFORMATION

ANTS

Yes, ants. The BVI has tiny, tiny little ants that can appear in a millisecond around anything they consider food, including toothpaste. Bring little baggies.

ARRIVING AND DEPARTING

American flies direct from many U.S. cities to San Juan, and connects with American Eagle flights to the little Tortola/Beef Island Airport. Delta and Continental offer a few connections through San Juan and also St. Thomas. If you are coming from the U.K., the best connection is British Airways to Antigua and then LIAT to Tortola/Beef Island. If you are connecting to American Eagle in San Juan, it is important that you get to your American Eagle gate early, because at the gate you will get onto a bus and be taken out to your plane. When you book a flight to the BVI you will almost always be routed through San Juan, with a connecting flight to the BVI. However, if you plan to stay on the western end of Tortola or on Jost Van Dyke, there is another (often easier) option. You can fly to St. Thomas (nonstop from major cities or via good connections in Miami) and take a 45 minute ferry ride to Tortola's West End *(Fast Ferry 340.777.2800, Smith's Ferry 340.775.7292, Native Son 340.774.8685, or go to www.stthomasthisweek.com for schedules)*. Ferries to Tortola depart from Charlotte Amalie, five minutes from the airport. (At Red Hook/East End, 30 minutes from the airport, ferries also leave for Tortola and Jost Van Dyke.) If your ferry connection is tight, tell the airport taxi coordinator and he will speed you into a taxi. If you are traveling to Virgin Gorda, you can fly to Beef Island and take the North Sound Express *(reservations necessary, see page 139)*, which goes to Leverick Bay and Bitter End (and The Valley if requested) from Trellis Bay, a three-minute cab ride from the airport. If you are going to Anegada, you can catch a flight from Beef Island *(see page 18)*. Biras Creek, Marina Cay, Little Dix Bay, and Peter Island have private ferries from Trellis Bay. **Dohm's Water Taxi** *(340.775.6501)* can arrange for a private taxi from the St. Thomas airport to the East End of St. Thomas, and then transport you in their comfortable catamarans to your island of choice. **Island Helicopters** *(284.499.2663)* offers private pick-ups from San Juan and St. Thomas to Anegada, Necker, Tortola, and Virgin Gorda.

Documents

U.S. citizens must have a valid passport to enter the BVI and to return to the U.S.

Entering the BVI

You clear immigration and customs at the airport, West End, Road Town, or Jost Van Dyke. Keep the little piece of paper they stick in your passport. It's collected when you leave the BVI (but don't panic if you lose it). Don't bring drugs into the BVI. This is a serious offense.

Exiting the BVI

There is a $10 per person departure tax at the airport; pay at the separate window way to the right of check in ($5 if you leave by boat). If you fly to San Juan, this is where you will clear customs into the U.S. Be prepared for one of the world's longest airport walks. When you finally get to the escalators, you will see elevators also, which are quicker if it is crowded. If you fly from the BVI to St. Thomas, this is where you will clear and after you check your baggage you collect it again to go through customs. If you depart via ferry from the BVI to St. Thomas you will clear at St. John and clear again at the St. Thomas airport.

Luggage

It is easiest to check it all the way through but bring a carryon with your bathing suit and whatever else you might need for one night because a small amount of luggage always ends up somewhere else and it won't get back to you for a day. To be extra safe, check your luggage only to San Juan (or St. Thomas) and recheck it for your flight to the BVI.

You Must Reconfirm Your Flight

American Airlines *(284.495.2559)*, Continental *(800.231.0856)*, Delta *(800.221.1212)*.

ATMS AND BANKS

On Tortola in Road Town you'll find FirstBank, Banco Popular, and Scotiabank, all with ATMs. There is also an ATM at Soper's Hole and two at Cane Garden Bay. In The Valley on Virgin Gorda, there is a FirstBank with an ATM near Yacht Harbour and an ATM at Yacht Harbour. On Jost Van Dyke, there is an ATM at the Jost Van Dyke Grocery in Great Harbour. BVI ATMs are often on the blink, so don't count on getting cash from them.

CAR RENTALS

Cars can be rented on Anegada *(see page 19)*, Jost Van Dyke *(see page 36)*, Tortola *(see page 65)*, and Virgin Gorda *(see page 106)* and run about $60 a day. If you are staying at a resort, you may find it easier to get there first and then rent a car. Almost all rental agencies will pick you up and some resorts have rental agencies on the premises. Some roads are rugged so always be sure that your rental car has a spare tire, jack, and tire-changing tools.

CRIME

It's rare on Tortola, and exceedingly rare on other British Virgin Islands. However, there's no point in creating temptation, so don't leave your wallet or an expensive camera lying about in your room or in your car. Lock doors on Tortola and in The Valley on Virgin Gorda.

CURRENCY, CREDIT CARDS, TAXES, AND TIPPING

The currency is the U.S. dollar. Most establishments take credit cards but you will encounter some that take only cash, so bring some cash or Traveler's Checks. Some establishments refuse to take American Express so be sure to bring a MasterCard or Visa. There is no sales tax but there is a 7% hotel tax and most hotels add a 10-13% service charge. Restaurant policies vary, and if no service is added, tip as you would in the States (15%-20%); if 10% service is added, make up the difference to get to 15%-20%; if 15% service is added, only add more if you want to. Most restaurants clearly state on the menu and on the bill whether or not a service charge is included. If you are at all unsure, just ask.

LODGING

Be prepared that even the fanciest lodging in the BVI may not provide service, cuisine, and amenities comparable to a full-service, luxury stateside resort. This is not a complaint, but rather a caution. The hotel is "in the islands, mon." Parts needed to make a repair or even ingredients needed to prepare certain meals may have missed the boat today. Relax. The trade-off is no lines, no rush, no crowds, no need to "reserve" your beach chair (there are always plenty). Go with the flow, look around you, enjoy the view.

POISONOUS FRUITS

Some fruits and berries in the BVI are poisonous. Do not eat anything off a tree or bush unless you are absolutely sure you know what it is.

PUBLIC HOLIDAYS

Major BVI holidays are New Years Day, Commonwealth Day (2nd Monday in March), Good Friday, Easter Sunday, Easter Monday, Whit Monday (50 days after Easter), Sovereign's Birthday (June 11), Territory Day (July 1), August Festival (first two weeks of August, dates vary year-to-year), St. Ursula's Day (around October 21), Christmas Day, and Boxing Day (December 26). Banks and virtually all shops will be closed on these days. If a holiday falls on a Sunday, then count on the next Monday being a holiday, too.

TAXIS

In the BVI, it is expected that passengers share taxis. When you are picked up at the airport or ferry, or even going into town from a resort, it is normal to share a taxi with people you don't know. Not only is this how the taxi driver can make a living, but it also enables a limited fleet of taxis to take everyone everywhere they need to go pretty much when they need to go there. (If three couples at the airport all waited for separate taxis, it would take much longer for many to get where they were going, since the same few taxis would be driving back and forth.) An advantage to passengers is that you can all share information (where did you eat, what is it like where you are staying, etc.). If you are looking for a taxi and one goes by with or without passengers in it, call out your destination and the driver will stop, provided he or she is going that way. If you get a chance, talk to the drivers. Many have lived all over the world. For taxi information, see page 19 for Anegada, page 36 for Jost Van Dyke, page 65 for Tortola, and page 106 for Virgin Gorda.

TELEPHONES, CELL PHONES, INTERNET, AND E-MAIL

The area code for the BVI is 284 (which is easy to remember because it is BVI). When you are in the BVI, use the seven-digit telephone number. Lots of local establishments have cell phones (boat trips, taxi drivers, almost everyone on Jost Van Dyke) but they are sometimes "out of range" even though they aren't. Just try again later. Your stateside cell phone probably will not work in the BVI unless it is a quadband GSM and then it must be activated by your provider (it may work unactivated on the eastern part of Jost Van Dyke). For Cingular call 1-866.246.4852 or go to www.cingular.com. For Verizon call 1.800.922.0204. Once in the BVI, you can go to Communications Products (284.494.1555) in Road Town (east of Pusser's on Main Street) to rent a cell phone. If you can bear it (and many do) just turn off your phone and enjoy the delightful novelty of being unreachable. In an emergency you can always be reached at your hotel or on a boat. Also most hotels provide a computer in the lobby so guests can access the Internet. *(For Internet cafes, see page 101.)*

TELEPHONING TO THE U.S. FROM THE BVI

If you don't have a working cell phone, there are several ways to call the U.S. from the BVI, most are expensive, and sometimes none of them work. If you get stuck, try again later. Sometimes dialing direct from your hotel is the cheapest way to call (ask the front desk what the rate is; rates vary greatly from hotel to hotel and sometimes it's best to try a call and then see what it costs). Dial 1-800-872-2881 for ATT (you can use your AT&T card or a major credit card) but sometimes this number will only connect you with Cable & Wireless and the call will be outrageously expensive (about $15 for the first minute, $3 for each additional minute). Dial 1-800-225-5872 or dial 111 or dial 115 and use a major credit card, but beware the cost if you get a Cable & Wireless operator. Coin phone booths say you can dial long distance from them but you almost always can't (they often won't work locally either).

TIME

The BVI is on Atlantic Standard Time (one hour ahead of Eastern Standard Time and the same time as Eastern Daylight Saving Time).

WEATHER

People tend to assume that the farther south one goes, the hotter it is. Not true! The BVI daytime temperatures hover around 75 degrees in the winter, 85 degrees in the summer and the trade winds almost always blow. New York City can be hotter in August than the BVI!

WHAT TO BRING

Sunscreen (the BVI are only 18 degrees from the equator and the sun is strong all year long), a little stick of bug repellent that you can keep in a pocket or purse, casual clothes. In the evening at the nicer restaurants on Tortola and Virgin Gorda, casual elegant resortwear is appropriate, including long pants and collared shirts for men. If you are staying on Jost Van Dyke, Anegada, or Cooper Island then you only need very casual clothes. Bring sturdy shoes if you want to hike and you might want a light sweater as evenings can be cool any time of year. You can always find a substitute but if you are particular about brands, bring enough shampoo, deodorant, etc. Bring a little flashlight. Paths are often not well lighted.

KEY TO RESTAURANT SYMBOLS

"B" and "L" and "D" appear at the end of restaurant descriptions and indicate whether the establishment is open for breakfast, lunch, and/or dinner. Meal prices are similar to those in a large U.S. city. Dollar symbols indicate price ranges. Lobster is always expensive and appetizers and desserts can add surprising amounts to a bill.

$ = INEXPENSIVE $$ = MODERATE $$$ = EXPENSIVE

FERRY SCHEDULES

Bear in mind that ferries can leave a little early or a little late. Also it is good advice to take the ferry that "looks like it is going soon" even if it is scheduled for a later departure than a ferry run by a competing company. For this reason, it makes sense to buy one-way rather than round-trip tickets.

BETWEEN ANEGADA AND TORTOLA
BETWEEN ANEGADA AND VIRGIN GORDA

Smith's Ferry (284.494.4454, 284.494.2355) runs ferrry service betweeen Anegada and Tortola. Virgin Gorda trips to Anegada are by reservation only and leave The Valley on Virgin Gorda at 7:30 am and leave Anegada at 5 pm.

From Road Town, Tortola (Monday, Wednesday, Friday)	From Anegada
7 am	8:30 am
3:30 pm	5 pm

BETWEEN TORTOLA AND JOST VAN DYKE

New Horizon (284.495.9278) ferries take 25-30 minutes to reach Great Harbor, Jost Van Dyke. The fare each way is $12. There is no ticket office. You pay on board. Just look for the boat, and be sure to get on when someone starts untying the lines. Departure time can be somewhat before or after the scheduled time. Sometimes on season on weekends or whenever enough people ask, there is a dinner ferry which leaves West End at 6:30 pm and returns later in the evening. Call if you're interested.

From West End, Tortola	From Jost Van Dyke
8 am (Mon.-Fri.)	7 am (Mon.-Fri)
9 am (Sat.-Sun.)	8 am (Sat.-Sun.)
10 am (Mon.-Fri.)	9 (Mon.-Fri.)
1 pm	9:30 (Sat.-Sun.)
4 pm	12 noon
6 pm	2 pm
	5 pm

BETWEEN TORTOLA AND COOPER ISLAND

Extremely limited ferry service runs between Cooper Island and Prospect Reef Marina just outside of Road Town, Tortola. Schedules are subject to change, so please call *(284.495.9084)*. Fare is $15 each way. (Free for hotel guests on weekly package.)

Monday, Wednesday, Friday

From Cooper	From Prospect Reef
7:30 am	8:30 am
4:30 pm	5:30 pm

BETWEEN TORTOLA AND VIRGIN GORDA (THE VALLEY)

In Tortola, ferries leave from the ferry docks in Road Town (across from Pusser's). In The Valley, ferries leave from the public dock just north (and within walking distance) of the Virgin Gorda Yacht Harbour. The fare is $10 each way and takes about 35 minutes.

on SPEEDY'S FERRIES *(284.495-5240)*

From Virgin Gorda	From Road Town
6:30 am (Tues., Thurs.)	9 am
8 am	10 am (Tues., Thurs.)
10 am	10:30 am
11:30 am	12 noon
12:30 pm	1:30 pm
2:45 pm (Tues., Thurs.)	4:30 pm
3:30 pm	5:15 pm (Sun.)
4:30 pm (Sun.)	6 pm (Mon., Fri.)
5 pm (Mon., Fri.)	6:15 pm (Tues., Thurs.)
6 pm (Wed., Sat.)	6:45 pm (Wed., Sat.)
10:30 pm (Wed., Sat.)	11 pm (Wed., Sat.)

on SMITH'S FERRIES *(284.495-4495)*

From Road Town	From Virgin Gorda
7 am (Mon-Sat)	7:50 am (Mon-Sat)
8:50 am	10:15 am
12:30 pm	2:15 pm (Mon.-Fri.)
3:15 pm (Mon-Fri)	3 pm (Sat.-Sun.)
4:15 pm (Sat, Sun)	4 pm (Mon.-Fri.)
	5 pm (Sat.-Sun.)

BETWEEN TORTOLA AND VIRGIN GORDA

The North Sound Express *(284.495-2138)* runs between Trellis Bay (on Beef Island past the airport) and Leverick Bay and the Bitter End on North Sound. The trip takes 30 minutes (45 if there is a stop at The Valley) and is $40 round-trip. Advance reservations are absolutely essential and departure times are subject to change, particularly from The Valley. Pick-up at Leverick Bay is 15 minutes prior to Bitter End pick-up. (Virgin Gorda has no ticket offices. Stand at the end of the dock to be sure the pilot sees you at these departures.)

From Tortola/Beef Island	From The Valley	From Bitter End
8:15 am	8:30 am	6:45 am
11:15 am	11:30 am	9 am
1:45 pm	4:30 pm	12 noon
4:15 pm		3:15 pm
6 pm		5 pm
8 pm ($25 one-way)		

BETWEEN TORTOLA AND MARINA CAY

The trip takes about 10 minutes and is free. Ferries leave from the little dock near the Trellis Bay Market which is a bit east of the Beef Island airport.

From Beef Island	From Marina Cay
10:30 am	10:15 am
11:30 am	11:15 am
12:30 pm	12:15 pm
3:00 pm	2:45 pm
4:00 pm	3:45 pm
5:00 pm	4:45 pm
6:00 pm	5:45 pm
7:00 pm	6:45 pm
	(later runs for restaurant guests)

BETWEEN TORTOLA AND PETER ISLAND

The trip takes about 30 minutes. Ferries leave from the resort's private dock (which many still call the CSY Dock) which is on the east side of Road Town Harbour. The fare is $15.00 per person. Fares are waived for those who have dinner reservations at Peter Island.

From Road Town	From Peter Island
7:00 am	8:00 am
8:30 am	9:00 am
10:00 am	11:30 am
12 noon	1:30 pm
2:00 pm	2:30 pm
3:30 pm	4:30 pm
5:30 pm	6:00 pm
6:30 pm	7:30 pm
8:00 pm	10:00 pm
10:30 pm	11:30 pm

BETWEEN GUN CREEK, VIRGIN GORDA AND THE BITTER END YACHT CLUB (VIRGIN GORDA) AND SABA ROCK

The trip between Gun Creek and Bitter End takes about 10 minutes and is free. At Gun Creek, the little wooden Bitter End ferry leaves from the dock. You can grab a beer or a soda from the Last Stop Bar across the street. And don't worry if there's not a soul around or a boat in sight. The ferry will appear! The ferry leaves Gun Creek every hour on the 1/2 hour beginning at 6:30 am and ending at 10:30 pm. The ferry leaves Bitter End every hour on the hour beginning at 6 am and ending at 11 pm. **Saba Rock** has a ferry, too. Call for schedules *(284.495.7711)*.

BETWEEN THE USVI AND THE BVI

Ferries leave from Charlotte Amalie, St. Thomas for West End and Road Town on Tortola and The Valley on Virgin Gorda. (Some ferries scheduled just for West End actually go on to Road Town. If you care, ask at the dock.) Ferries leave from Red Hook (East End), St. Thomas for West End, Tortola; for Jost Van Dyke (Fri.-Sun.); and for Virgin Gorda (Thurs., Sun.). The best sources for current ferry schedules between the USVI and the BVI are stthomasthisweek.com and www.bviwelcome.com.

INDEX

ABOUT THE AUTHORS

Since escaping from corporate life in Manhattan, husband and wife team Pam Acheson and Dick Myers have spent the last 15 years living in and exploring the Virgin Islands and Florida. Between them they have authored, written, and contributed to over 60 books, written articles for many national and international magazines, and have been featured guests on dozens of television and radio shows throughout the United States and the Caribbean. Their extremely knowledgeable, personal, reader-friendly guides to the U.S. Virgin Islands, the British Virgin Islands, and romantic Florida perennially rank among the best sellers in the world for these destinations. They reside in the Virgin Islands and Florida...and quite enjoy visiting Manhattan.